Super Prest

Lancashire United

A Centenary Celebration
1905–2005

Eric Ogden

additional research and layout

John A Senior

© 2006 Venture Publications Ltd

ISBN 1905 304 12 9
ISBN 978 1905 304 129

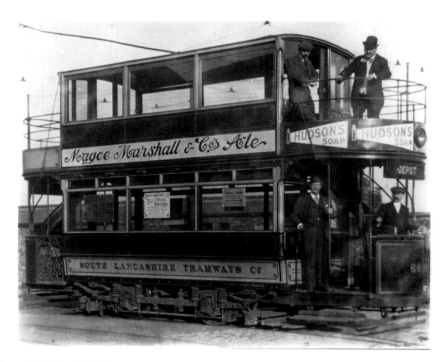

SLT car No. 60 in original condition, one of 24 single-truck top-covered cars costing £545 each in 1906.
Unfortunately, many of SLT's records were lost in the drive for salvage during the Second World War. This
led to conflicting reports about the builder of this batch, numbered 59-82. Mr. Edwardes is reported as
stating that they were built by the United Electric Car Co. Ltd. of Preston, while contemporary newspaper
reports state that some were built by the Brush Electrical Engineering Co. Ltd. and some by UEC. Expert
opinion is that the cars display Brush features, certainly Nos. 59-72. All the cars were top-covered from new
but with roofless open canopies. This feature is evident in the illustration of No. 60 with JR Salter, General
Manager, at the controls while EH Edwardes, Power Station Engineer, stands at the left on the upper-deck.

South Lancashire Tramways Company.

9, North John Street

Liverpool.

TELEGRAMS,
"TRACTORY, LIVERPOOL".

TELEPHONE № 7927, CENTRAL.

SECRETARY,
H. P. CONIBEAR.

Introduction

W hy a third book on LUT? First, January 2006 marks the centenary of the inaugural meeting after the formation in December 1905 of the original Lancashire United Tramways company and it is felt that this unusual and individualistic business, which developed to become Britain's largest independent bus operator, should be recognised by a commemorative publication now that it is no longer in existence.

Second, since the appearance of the author's previous work on this subject in 1985 the opportunity has been taken to carry out further research into the company's antecedents and the early years of its history. Papers at Companies House, together with transcripts of the company minutes which became available after the publication of the 1985 book, various legal and business directories and other papers, all used in conjunction with trade magazines and year books of the times, have thrown new light on the subject.

Third, the author made a plea in his 1974 book that the personal aspect of road passenger transport history should be given greater consideration by future transport historians. Again and again it becomes apparent to the student of road passenger transport undertakings that such organisations are very often shaped and characterised by the powerful personalities of their managers. Nowhere was this more true than with LUT's Ned Edwardes.

We have discovered the backgrounds of the founding directors which reveal them to be men of vision, capability and expertise in their various fields of finance, telegraphy, electrical engineering, horse and electric tramway construction, manufacturing, accountancy and law which enabled them to succeed after many setbacks in a new and competitive industry.

There is more to tell than can be contained in a celebratory publication of this nature and it may be possible in the future to produce a further updated hardback full history. In the meantime, author and publisher hope that enough of the story has been included to whet the appetite of all who are interested in road passenger transport history, and in South Lancashire, while giving a flavour of what was a most unusual company. Now, after the new research, we have a better understanding as to why it was so remarkable.

The South Lancashire Tramways Company – and the other antecedents

Lancashire United Transport Ltd. had its origins in the Lancashire Light Railways Company Ltd., formed on 21st April 1898 with a capital of £50,000 and registered office at 12 St. John's Lane, Liverpool. This company was granted a light railway order which permitted it to construct a tramway. The promoters were the brothers Jacob Atherton (1852-1921) of Gateacre and James Basnett Atherton of Manhattan House, Rainhill. The brothers had business interests in Australia and the USA, and on their return from America in 1890 they formed the British Insulated Wire Company Ltd. in Prescot. They were obviously interested in electricity supply and electric tramways and in Australia were connected with the Electric Supply Company of Victoria Ltd., and the Electric Supply Company of Western Australia Ltd., both of which had acquired the tramway systems of Bendigo and Ballarat, converting them to electric operation.

The brothers demonstrated to the press a small electric single-deck tram on a short length of track using the conduit system on 9th March 1897 at their Prescot factory.

The gap between Prescot and the rest of the South Lancashire tramway system was served by the earlier St Helens & District Tramways Company Ltd. St Helens Corporation acquired ownership of this company on 1st April 1897 while operation was taken over by a new company entitled the New St Helens & District Tramways Company Ltd. promoted by Jacob and James Atherton and registered on 4th November 1898. The Secretary of the original St Helens company, Mr G Saies, was appointed Secretary of the New St Helens company, the Lancashire Light Railways Company and several of the other companies in which the Athertons were involved.

The South Lancashire Tramways Company was formed by Act of Parliament (and therefore was without the word 'limited' in its title) on 6th August 1900 which authorised construction of electric tramways over a wide area between St. Helens and Manchester, with the intention of linking Liverpool and Manchester. The original Bill provided for 79 miles of tramway passing through 20 local authority areas. In the event only 32 miles were constructed, largely due to

The precursor companies' involvement with tramways began with the New St Helens Company, as mentioned in the text, and the sketch map below indicates the extent of the tramway running lines.

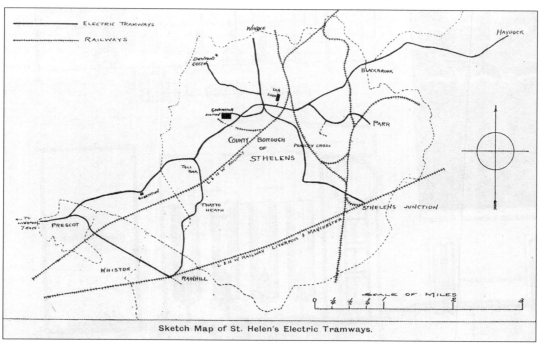

Sketch Map of St. Helen's Electric Tramways.

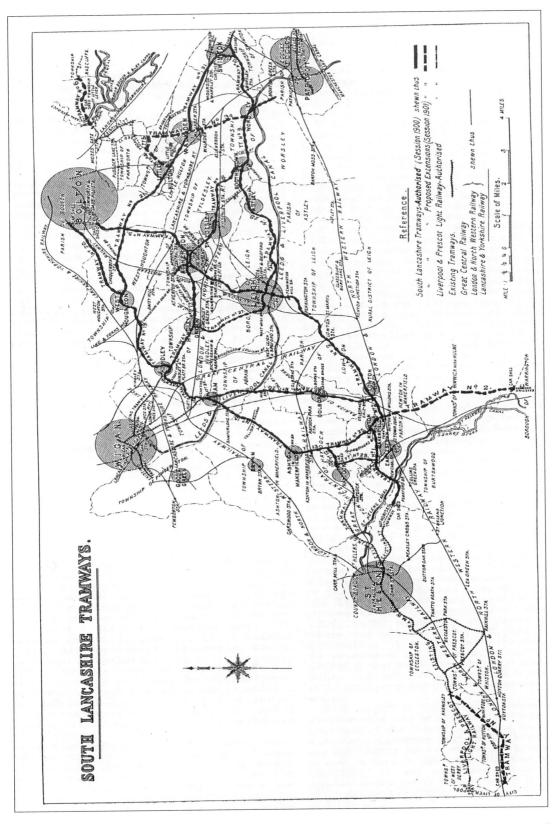

SOUTH LANCASHIRE TRAMWAYS.

The New St Helens Company cars, above, were distinctive with their Mozeley screens to protect the driver from the elements at a time when most other operators still left him exposed to their mercy – as indeed did South Lancashire and Lancashire United with their cars right to the end of operation in December 1933. Notice that the screen does not enclose the staircase. *(GLC)*

A quite different design of SLT car is seen below at the Hulton Arms Hotel, Hulton Lane Ends. Number 49 had previously been owned by Farnworth UDC and passed to Lancashire United Tramways in 1906 when the company purchased the Farnworth system. Note the very shallow upper-deck decency panels and the reversed staircases which restricted the driver's view.

subsidence from the extensive coal mining operations in the area damaging such track as had been laid and raising questions as to the wisdom of laying further rails. The Act gave the company powers to carry parcels between 11 pm and 5 am when passenger traffic was not operating, to supply electric power to local authorities and other commercial users such as cotton mills, and to erect street lighting. The parcels service, however, proved to be unremunerative and was discontinued after a few months. It had been intended also to make use of the Cheshire Lines Committee's rail lines, through interchange at its railway stations; the CLC was part-owned by the Great Central Railway. A separate company, the South Lancashire Electric Supply Company Ltd., was formed on 29th June 1900 for the purpose of supplying electricity though, in fact, it never traded and was struck off the Register of Joint Stock Companies after December 1931.

The South Lancashire Electric Traction and Power Company Ltd. was formed on 29th November 1900 to acquire the Lancashire Light Railways Company Ltd., the South Lancashire Tramways Company, the South Lancashire Electric Supply Company Ltd., and the New St Helens & District Tramways Company Ltd. thus becoming the parent company of the group with four subsidiary companies. James and Jacob Atherton were directors together with the Hon. Arthur Stanley MP (third son of the then 16th Lord Derby); the Hon. George Stanley; Joseph Beecham, (Chairman of the St Helens Corporation Lighting and Tramway Committee and later an Alderman of that town); EK Muspratt, (a Director and Chairman of British Insulated & Helsby Cables Ltd., and a Director of, amongst other companies, the two Australian tramways mentioned above together with the Midland Electric Corporation (1900) Ltd. of which he was also Chairman) whilst Sir John Willox, proprietor of the Liverpool Courier, was SLT's Chairman. The Hon. Arthur Stanley succeeded Willox as Chairman in 1902. By 1904, if not earlier, CE Maples of Ormskirk, who was a Director of the Birkenhead & Chester Tramways Company Ltd., was also on the board of the four 'Atherton' companies. The registered office continued at 12 St. John's Lane, Liverpool until 1904 when it was moved to the Prudential Assurance building at 9 North John Street. Henry Percy Conibear was appointed Secretary to all five

companies when the Atherton brothers departed at the time of the company's reconstruction in 1905. John Ruffell Salter, previously assistant engineer to Sir Clifton Robinson of London United Tramways, was appointed initially as SLT's engineer (see page 11), but by February 1906 was General Manager of both the SLT and LUT companies, and Edward Henry Edwardes (who had also been with the London United company) was appointed power station engineer.

The power station at Howe Bridge, between Atherton and Leigh and built in 1901/2, was supervised by constructional engineers Kincaid, Walker and Manville of London. The first 50 trams, each providing 55 seats, were built by

The ECC was one of many organisations using Dashwood House in the City of London as its Head Office, as shown in the advertisement below. The works and foundry were located in Wolverhampton and the company used Ferranti Ltd as supplier of generators in many of its contracts. Mr Ferranti was linked with the Atherton brothers through the patent he purchased for paper insulation of copper wire, and his position as a director in their Helsby company. His company became an LUT shareholder in the reorganisation after liquidation, having supplied the Howe Bridge generating equipment. Dashwood House, with the many companies within its confines, was much more significant to our narrative, however, as the unfolding story on page 9 reveals.

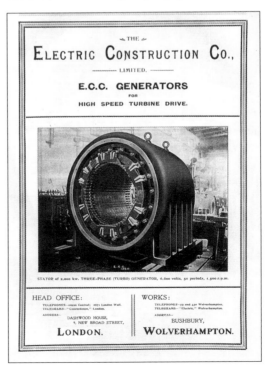

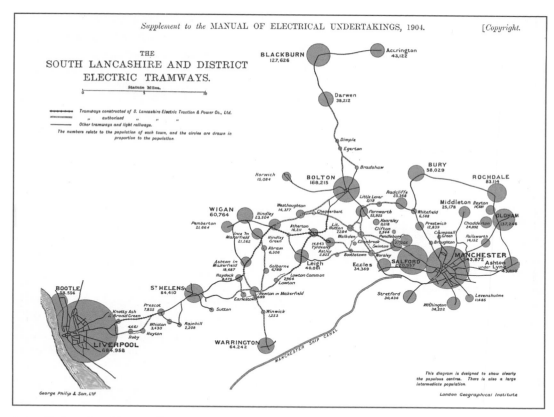

THE
SOUTH LANCASHIRE AND DISTRICT
ELECTRIC TRAMWAYS.

A simplified version of the map illustrated on page five, showing how SLT's lines connected with those of other operators between Manchester, Bolton and Liverpool.

GF Milnes & Co. of Hadley, Shropshire using Belgian electrical equipment, at a cost of £610 each. The track and overhead was expected to be completed at a quoted price of £21,544 but the final cost turned out to be three times this amount. The girder rail, in 45ft. lengths, came from Ougrée in Belgium, the pointwork from Hadfields Steel Foundry Co. of Sheffield and the crossings from Askham Bros. and Wilson Ltd. The overhead wire was produced by the Athertons' British Insulated Wire Co. Ltd., which became part of British Insulated Helsby Cables Ltd. (later British Insulated Callender's Cables Ltd. [BICC]). The German company Krauss & Co., through its British Bristol-based subsidiary, laid the track and Messrs Blackwell erected the poles and overhead wire. Construction work began at Four Lane Ends in October 1901 (see the photograph on page 6).

Having spent £1,006,000 on constructing the tramway system, the South Lancashire Electric Traction and Power Company Ltd. found itself in

financial difficulties. On 4th July 1904 an application was made to the Manchester Chancery Court by Krauss & Co., the permanent way constructors, for the appointment of receivers. The court appointed two SLT Directors, Mr JR Salter and Mr JM Henderson, as joint receivers and managers. An extraordinary meeting of the company on 7th October 1904 decided that the company should go into voluntary liquidation with the object of facilitating reconstruction. With no prospect of any return for the shareholders being likely in the future, the Hon. Arthur Stanley started a subscription fund for the formation of a new company which duly became entitled Lancashire United Tramways Ltd, as explained on page 10.

It is appropriate at this point to consider just how much progress had been made up to 1905 since liquidation perhaps implies failure whereas much had actually been achieved. The generating station at Howe Bridge had been built, and was operational and supplying power profitably to some of the local authorities. Two car sheds had been built, at Howe Bridge, and Platt Bridge, Hindley. The latter, however, was used only for rebuilding tramcar bodies until 1927 when trams operated from there in the run up to the introduction of trolleybuses in 1930. Track had been laid and was in use, and a fleet of 46 trams had been delivered and put into service. Further tramway extensions were planned and the necessary authorisations obtained.

Two main problems had been encountered. The cost of track construction, as already mentioned, had escalated owing to the nature of the roads with subsidence due to the extraction of the coal below them. Since much of the land belonged to Lord Derby, the Chairman's father, this must have given rise to some interesting conversations between father and son! The other problem was the economy, in particular the cotton trade, which at the time was in a parlous state. Since many of the company's potential passengers who normally worked in the local textile mills were unemployed, the revenue from tramway operation was down on predictions, and sales of electricity to those same mills would also have been below expectations.

While the situation appeared to be desperate, the potential was there for those who could keep their heads. Arthur Stanley was just such a man. Having grown up in a financial background (his father had been Financial Secretary to the Treasury) he was used to dealing with financiers, and used Dashwood House as his London office. Here, he would have met the financier John Soame Austen whose wide experience derived from his involvement in many companies and from being a Government stockbroker. Undoubtedly, Stanley turned to him for help and advice. Mr Austen became a director of LUT in 1906, representing the minority interest held by the British Electric Traction Company Ltd. (BET). In June 1909 it was reported that the Hon. Arthur Stanley, who had recently joined the board of BET, had retired from it pending determination of a business in which he had a conflicting interest. This may have been through possible connection with the Electric Construction Company, which, as seen on page 7, was based at Dashwood House where Arthur Stanley and JS Austen shared several business interests. The conflict could then have been with the National Electric Construction Company in which BET had an interest and would eventually be the outright owner.

Motor bus operation commenced on 23rd March 1906 with a service from Leigh town centre to Westleigh St. Pauls, a distance of about one and a half miles. On Sundays this continued to Leigh Cemetery on the opposite side of the town. A second route, from Lowton St. Mary's tram terminus to Newton in Makerfield, commenced on 6th July 1906. On the same date SLT commenced running tramcars from the Leigh boundary to Lowton St. Mary's station to link up with the Great Central Railway system. Three 14 hp Scott-Stirling buses were ordered and the Leigh service at first must have been operated solely by the first to be delivered. It was reported on 4th April 1906 by the General Manager (JR Salter, General Manager of SLT who was appointed to LUT in February 1906) that the other two were ready for delivery at a total cost of £1,100.

The buses were built by the Scott-Stirling Motor Company Ltd. Stirling was an early bus builder based in Hamilton, Scotland. The company ran into difficulties and its buses, by then known as Scott-Stirling, were subsequently assembled at Twickenham, Middlesex and the manufacturer supplied the London Power Omnibus Company Ltd. with over 60 vehicles. Most bodies on Scott-Stirling buses were built by the Brush Electrical Engineering Company Ltd., a subsidiary of BET. By 1907 both the London Power Omnibus Company and Scott-Stirling had disappeared. LUT's vehicles operated for only about three months when it was decided that they were unsuitable for the work required of them and were "very expensive" to run (according to Arthur Stanley) and so were withdrawn. It is apparent that the Stanley family had many business interests, and one of the London Power Omnibus Company's Directors was Ferdinand Stanley, Arthur's immediate younger brother. The next younger brother was a Director of the Electric Landaulette Company Ltd.

In the meantime, Mr Salter announced in May 1906 that he was considering linking Bolton and Manchester with motor buses, but this was not to be in his time. The three motor buses were returned to the makers and they then passed to the Ortona Company of Cambridge, later to be converted to double deckers. LUT was charged £150 for the repainting and modification of the two vehicles. Arthur Stanley stated that experience of the motor buses showed that they were not likely to enter into competition with the Company's tramways.

Soon afterwards, in September 1906, SLT's new line from Boothstown to Winton was opened, thus

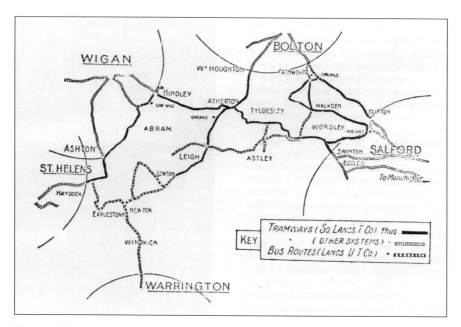

The start of bus operation in 1906 with three Scott-Stirling single-deckers has been mentioned on page 9. They were not sufficiently reliable and the services on which they had been used, shown above, were withdrawn by October of that year. It is quite clear from the Minutes that the buses must have been ordered by SLEP&T before LUT was set up and we now know that through the link between Arthur Stanley and and his brother Ferdinand Stanley with Sir Robert Dashwood in the London Power Omnibus Company, these vehicles had actually previously operated in London, but were withdrawn as being too small for potential traffic.

They may well have been assembled in Twickenham, London, where Scott-Stirling was based for some months, and close to the depot of the other LUT company, London United Tramways.

The three vehicles were duly re-registered before operating in Lancashire and after being withdrawn by Lancashire United Tramways, were returned to the manufacturer via the dealer. The three vehicles were eventually sold to the Ortona Company of Cambridge. Ortona later added open top decks to the buses, and in that form they ran until they were withdrawn in 1914. This view shows two of the trio in service, soon after delivery to Ortona. Lancashire United Tramways had been obliged to pay £150 to cover the cost of modifications and repainting as a condition for withdrawing from its commitment to purchase. *(CC)*

forming a connecting link in the tramways from Liverpool Pier Head, via Wigan and Eccles, to the centre of Manchester. The trade press remarked that the journey to "Cottonopolis" could now be made "with a few changes!"

In their first report, covering the period to 31st December 1906, the Directors explained the relationship between LUT and its subsidiary companies. The new company owned the whole of the issued share capital of the South Lancashire Transport Company and the Lancashire Light Railways Company Ltd. and over 80% of the shares of the New St. Helens & District Tramways Company Ltd., although these companies continued as the actual owners or lessees of the tramways and they were the operating companies. The South Lancashire Electric Traction and Power Company Ltd. had already been placed in voluntary liquidation. The traffic receipts went direct to the subsidiary companies and any profits made by them in the working of their respective systems were paid over to LUT as dividends on the share capital. LUT owned the depot and the generating station at Howe Bridge, the sub-stations and the car sheds. The net working profit for the period commencing 1st March 1906 amounted to £7,692 and after payment of debenture interest there was a balance of £317.

The offices of LUT and its subsidiary companies were transferred from Liverpool to a new building at Howe Bridge adjoining the depot in July 1906, thus bringing together the administrative and operational headquarters.

The accounts for 1907 were produced at the annual meeting held in London on 28th February 1908 with Mr JM Henderson presiding. Profit for the year was £12,789 and after payment of debenture interest there was a balance of £289. This amount, with the credit balance from the previous year, was written off against the disposal of the three Scott-Stirling motor buses. It was noted that receipts per tramcar mile had been steadily increasing since operations began. The accounts for 1908 showed an increase in profits of £3,685 over the previous year but it was stated that the results had been affected by a cotton strike.

LUT and its subsidiary companies suffered a severe blow with the death of General Manager John Ruffell Salter on 15th December 1910 at the early age of 35. He was regarded as "one of the best known and most capable managers and engineers in the North of England." An expert in tramway matters who had often appeared before Parliamentary Committees, he acted as consulting engineer for various other undertakings including London United Tramways before coming to SLT

Sir Arthur Stanley

John Soame Austen

The Hon. Arthur Stanley's many business interests included a Directorship of Parr's Bank, and later, when Parr's merged, a similar position with the Westminster Bank.

in 1901. Salter was born in London in 1875 and was educated at Kings College, London. In 1893 he became assistant to Professor John Hopkinson FRS, one of Britain's most distinguished scientists and electrical engineers. The latter, a member of the prominent Hopkinson family of Manchester, was killed at the age of 48 in 1898 in an Alpine climbing accident. His father, also John, was Mayor of Manchester in 1882, and his brother, Sir Alfred, was Professor of Law and Vice-Chancellor of Manchester University.

While working in Hopkinson's practice, Salter was engaged in tramway and electric lighting installations at Leeds, Liverpool, Sheffield and Crewe. Following the death of Hopkinson, John

Salter was appointed chief assistant engineer to James Clifton Robinson (later Sir Clifton) with responsibility for the initial electrical construction and equipment of London United Tramways and also for the electrification of the Bristol Tramways. On completion of the London assignment in 1901, as recorded, Salter moved to Atherton to join the fledgling but promising new organisation.

Contemporary reports speak of "Mr Salter's geniality and kindly disposition" and "a career which gave unusual promise." The funeral took place at Worsley and was attended by the Hon. Arthur Stanley, Mr EH Edwardes and several hundred of the company's employees. Eight motormen and conductors acted as bearers.

John Ruffell Salter

Edward Henry (Ned) Edwardes

The Lancashire United Tramways Ltd.

With help from friends and others in the City, the Hon. Arthur Stanley's fund raising was successful. The authorised capital was £200,000 in ordinary shares and £700,000 in debentures of which a total of £822,708 was issued. The new company was registered on 29th December 1905, its object being to take over the South Lancashire Electric Traction and Power Company Ltd. and its subsidiary companies from 1st March 1906. Its function was to control and co-ordinate the activities of its subsidiary companies. Stanley was appointed Chairman and the registered office remained at 9 North John Street, Liverpool. The Atherton brothers then disappeared from the scene. Jacob died in Torquay in 1921 having survived his elder brother by some years. Arthur Stanley was MP for Ormskirk from 1898 until he retired in 1918, having received a knighthood in 1917 for his work with the Red Cross. He remained Chairman of LUT until his death in 1947, having been at the helm for 45 years. This longevity was to be a hallmark of the LUT top management.

Undoubtedly, the financial well-being of the company, and its standing in the City, was, however, due to a man second only to Arthur Stanley, though one who kept a much lower profile. John Soame Austen was thus a notable appointment as a Director in June 1906. An investment broker, he was Managing Director of the Government Stocks & Other Securities Company Ltd., together with Directorships of companies with interests in finance, telegraphy, electrical generating and distribution, railways and tramways in Britain, South America, Spain and Asia; he was Chairman of many of these, having his office at the Omnium Company Ltd., 69 Dashwood House, 9 New Broad Street, London, where the LUT Directors' meetings were held in his office. Deputy to Emil Garcke of the British Electric Traction Group, he became BET Chairman when Garcke retired in 1920. He continued as a Director of LUT until his death at the age of 80 in January 1942. Dashwood House is named after a long-deceased and colourful relative of Sir Robert Dashwood, who, in 1899, was Chairman of the London Power Omnibus Company Ltd. with which the Hon. Arthur Stanley was also associated, as mentioned earlier.

At the first meeting at Dashwood House in the City of London on 2nd January 1906 other Directors appointed were Joseph Beecham, a paper merchant from St. Helens with business interests in the North Wales Power & Traction Company Ltd., and the St Helens Cable Company Ltd., being a Director of both those companies and also a member of the famous pill-making family which included Sir Thomas Beecham the musician, and Robert Watson, Secretary to the National Electric Construction Company Ltd. and also the Musselburgh Electric Tramways Company (of which he was later Manager until 1916) – his family were paper manufacturers from Linwood, near Paisley. In March 1906 Edwin Adam, an advocate from Edinburgh, was appointed a Director but he resigned the following month to be succeeded by his relative Alfred Adam, a barrister also from Edinburgh. Edwin was a co-Director of CE Maples in the Birkenhead & Chester Tramways Company Ltd., in addition to the Directorships he held in the four 'precursor' companies which came into LUT. In 1908 the board expressed its sympathy with Alfred on his bereavement; could this have been Edwin's

A company letterhead from 1920, showing Jacob R Holt as Secretary and the Secretary's Office now located at Atherton. Compare this with the earlier (SLT) version shown on page 2. Mr Holt went on to serve the Company for over 35 years.

The Lancashire United Tramways Limited.

TELEGRAMS,
"TRAMWAYS, ATHERTON."
TELEPHONE Nº 36.
SECRETARY.
J. R. HOLT.

Secretary's Office,

Atherton, Lancs.

demise? John Macdonald Henderson was another early Director. An accountant from London, he was Member of Parliament for West Aberdeenshire from 1906 until defeated in 1918 on boundary revisions. Henderson, a Ferranti man and a Director of the company which built the generators for the Howe Bridge power station, was also a Director of the South London Electric Supply Corporation in which the Atherton brothers had been involved. An LUT Director until his death in 1922, he was regarded by the Board as a very significant loss.

These details indicate the spread of interests of the Directors. They represent a variety of copper-based industries, including several telephone communication and manufacturing companies, cable manufacture with patented paper insulation, electrical generation, distribution and engineering, the law, finance and investment, transport in the form of steam railways and electric tramways, and also by motor bus. Additionally some were Members of Parliament, belonged to the landed gentry, or were entrepreneurs and philanthropists. The geographical spread is also noteworthy covering South Lancashire, Scotland and London.

It may be thought curious that a Lancashire company's monthly board meetings were held in the City of London in Dashwood House. It appears that this building, which was destroyed in the blitz, consisted of a terrace of large houses which had been converted into office accommodation for companies and individual businessmen. Many of these were involved in electricity generation and distribution and wireless telegraphy, both of which were rapidly developing industries at the time. Having become established in these industries, syndicates of businessmen naturally expanded their interests into the nascent electric tramway industry. Some had overseas interests, particularly in South America for copper production and trading for wire and cable, and Australia for electric tramway construction and operation. Located in the financial heart of the City of London, Dashwood House accommodated financiers with access to capital, Parliamentary promoters, and manufacturers, many of whom were relevant to the South Lancashire tramway enterprises. The occupants of Dashwood House operated an internal messenger service for transmission of documents within the building and to City institutions such as the Bank of England, the Stock Exchange and the Baltic and other exchanges within close proximity. Nearby, in Bartholomew Lane, was Parr's Bank Ltd., the LUT bank, of which Arthur Stanley was a director.

It is clear that JS Austen, in whose office the meetings were held, managed the finances of LUT. On occasions when he was not present at meetings the minutes state that "owing to the absence of Mr Austen, finance was not discussed."

That he was the key player where finance and forward planning was concerned is confirmed by the fact that rest of the Board had to travel from Liverpool, Atherton and Edinburgh every month, (twice in February), to attend the meetings in his office which allowed him to fit Lancashire United into his wide business portfolio.

Later in our story, when it became necessary to consider the General Manager's report in 1930 for the year 1931, forecasting a serious deficit each month as more trolleybuses and other associated conversion costs would be incurred to replace the last trams between Leigh and Bolton, the Minutes merely record 'that the matter of finding the necessary finance was left in the hands of Mr Austen'. Clearly they were very capable hands; clearly they needed to be.

From around 1908, or possibly earlier, the Annual and Extraordinary General Meetings were being held in Dashwood House, London. Room 104 must have been a Meeting Room; Room 69 was Mr Austen's office.

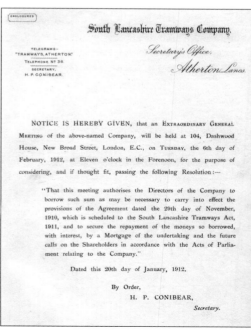

1910 – 1920

– unsettled times

In January 1911 Edward Henry Edwardes, power station engineer, was appointed General Manager in succession to Mr Salter, and went on to serve for another 45 years. At the same meeting in London, JM Henderson (Chairman in the absence of Stanley) stated that passenger receipts had again been affected by the unsatisfactory condition of the cotton industry. The number of consumers of energy, however, had increased and this area continued to be profitable. Further subsidence caused by coal mining had affected the tramway track resulting in an increase in reinstatement costs. From 1st January 1912 the generating station, car sheds, distributing stations and other land and buildings were transferred to SLT, an Act of Parliament sanctioning the transfer having been obtained. Also from 1912 Joseph Beecham appeared as Sir Joseph.

After the unsuccessful attempt to operate bus services in 1906, LUT tried again in 1914 with three Dennis 3-ton 28-seat charabancs. The cost was £750 each, and a garage to house them was erected at a cost of £700. The Government declared war with Germany in August 1914 and before LUT could make any real progress the new vehicles were requisitioned by the military and the chassis taken to Aldershot for Army use. Later in 1914 the General Manager was instructed to obtain tenders for three replacement chassis. The Daimler company was approached and tendered

£600 each for chassis without tyres but they were not to be delivered until the end of the war. After trying to expedite delivery in 1915 the Directors decided not to proceed on these terms and the charabanc bodies were sold later that year to the Trinity Garage Co. Ltd. of Halifax for £120.

The tramway workshops at Atherton were required by the Government to carry out production of munitions, initially as a 'filler' but from May 1915 onwards the local press was reporting that they were machining 18 lb. high-explosive shells at the rate of up to 1000 per week. This enforced concentration on munitions, however, proved to be to the detriment of tramway maintenance.

The sudden death of Sir Joseph Beecham was recorded in the minutes in November 1916. In the same year a bizarre use of SLT trams was the transport of prisoners of war from their 'camp' in a disused factory in Leigh to their places of work – doubtless for the war effort!

Throughout the war SLT continued to struggle to maintain its tram services, though some overdue repairs to the track and improvements to pointwork were accomplished. Staff numbers declined as hostilities continued and eventually, and not without grave misgivings, Edwardes gave in and allowed women to be employed as conductresses. Despite the absence of men away in the armed services the undertaking continued to be a prime mover of large numbers of people, mostly workers. Late in 1917 the Board congratulated Sir Arthur Stanley on the recent award of his knighthood which, as mentioned, was for his work with the Red Cross during WW1. In May 1918 the Secretary

The heavy engineering equipment needed to maintain a tramway, or railway, was also ideal for the manufacture of munitions and, accordingly, SLT, in common with many other operators, found itself working for the Government by making shell cases for the war effort. Note that most of the men have gone, and been replaced by women. Although the Treasury was a notoriously slow payer the eventual settlement would have gone some way towards replacing lost ticket and other revenue.

SLT was one of many heavy engineering organisations which played their part during 1914-1918 and it came under Government control in 1915. Here 18 lb. high explosive shells are seen after machining at Atherton. The volume gradually increased until production attained 1000 shells per week, but this work had a detrimental effect on tramway maintenance. Engineering and office staff from the GM downwards contributed to this additional vital contribution to the war effort.

reported that Parr's Bank had merged with the London County and Westminster Bank Ltd. Stanley was a director of both.

With the end of hostilities in November 1918 the Directors lost no time in agreeing to recommence motor charabanc operation, and the General Manager was authorised to obtain estimates for no less than 24 vehicles. As a result 24 x 40 hp chassis were ordered from Dennis Bros. Ltd. of Guildford at £888 each, and 24 charabanc bodies painted in torpedo grey were ordered from Charlesworth Motor Bodies Ltd. of Coventry at £265 each, a total of £1,153 per vehicle. Similar vehicles before the war cost around £750. It appears that the Dennis chassis were ex-War Department and were reconditioned by the makers. In addition a small Unic vehicle was purchased from this French manufacturer well-known as a builder of London taxis in the 1920s. The 1-ton pneumatic-tyred chassis carried a 14-seat body.

The Board resolved that Mr Gustav Roberts be appointed Liverpool manager for two years, and that a motor garage in Bentley Road, Liverpool be purchased for £4,500 from the Liverpool Carriage Co Ltd. Roberts was to bear the expenses of the office and staff and to agree not to run or have any interest in any other charabanc business in the area. It was further decided to let a portion of the garage to Roberts for five years but the purpose of this is not stated in the minutes.

The Dennis vehicles duly arrived and it was decided, due to the growth of the business, to order a further twelve, the unit price being £1516 reflecting the fact that these were as-new vehicles. At the same time five 14-seat Austin chassis were ordered. However, by the end of the year the General Manager had reported that the Austins could not be obtained so the order was transferred to Fiat for five 30-cwt chassis. On the back of the increased traffic and other business the first dividend on the ordinary shares was paid in 1919. Things were improving.

St Helens Corporation refused to renew the lease of its system when it expired and commenced operating itself from 1st October 1919. LUT purchased the 36 cars of the New St Helens and District Tramways Company Ltd. and put the company into liquidation. As the Liverpool and Prescot line was now isolated from the other tramways in the SLT group, that line was sold to Liverpool Corporation and the LLR Company was liquidated. The seven cars were transferred to SLT.

Also in October 1919, the GM reported on the purchase by Tourist Hotels Ltd. of the Ponsonby Arms Hotel at Llangollen. With a view to the expected postwar development of 'motor coach parties' and the catering involved, the Directors resolved that LUT should take up to 1,000 shares at £1 each in Tourist Hotels Ltd. In February 1920 it was agreed to take up another 1,000 £1 shares.

For some months after recommencing motor bus operation, only private hire and excursion traffic had been operated. Regular bus service began on 18th June 1920 with a route between the Lowton St. Mary's and Haydock tram termini, a six mile journey through Newton-le-Willows and Earlestown using new AEC buses. Two other buses operated in Liverpool carrying passengers for the North Atlantic Passenger Conference in that year. From now on development was rapid and services became more than feeders to tram routes. At this point the LUT fleet was about 40 vehicles and the SLT fleet contained about 50 trams. Mr HP Conibear resigned as Secretary on 31st August 1920 to be succeeded by Mr JR Holt; the latter gentleman would remain as Secretary until 1955.

Make-do-and-mend summed up wartime conditions in both conflicts, but here we see how lack of maintenance on the road, track and the tram itself was creating a situation whereby huge expenditure would be needed to return the system to its proper condition.

The advertisement below gives an indication of LUT's activities in the early 1920s. The Company faced stiff competition from small local operators who were willing to cut fares, often ruinously, to gain business as shown in the smaller illustration alongside. Needless to say Lancashire United was not a member of this association but the list of those companies which were members made for interesting reading.

Representative of the first post-WW1 charabancs is B 8772, one of 24 reconditioned ex-War Department Dennis 40 hp chassis with new 28-seat bodies by Charlesworth Motor Bodies Ltd. of Coventry. It is pictured at Worsley Courthouse which still stands in 2006. Note the maximum legal speed of 12 mph shown below the first door. The front seat passenger is thought to be the Chairman, the Hon. Arthur Stanley.

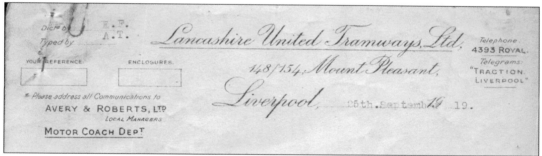

An Avery & Roberts letterhead from September 1919 showing the Liverpool address.

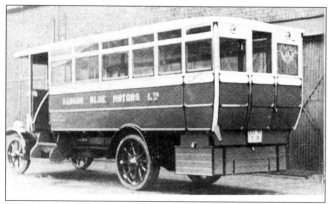

One of the two buses transferred to the Bangor Blue Motor Co. Ltd. in exchange for shares in that company in 1922. Dennis TB 1164 has been fitted with a new bus body of the 'boxy' type with projecting canopy as shown on page 25, but retains its solid tyres. It is pictured here at Atherton after repainting in Bangor Blue livery.

A line-up of several of the Dennis charabancs on an excursion from Liverpool to Llanrwst, North Wales in 1920. The party of 750 people covered 140 miles in the day. In March 1921 Mr Edwardes referred to these vehicles being used during a railway strike when they "behaved really handsomely between Liverpool, Manchester, Carlisle, Bradford, Huddersfield and even as far south as Southampton and Plymouth." The Dennis vehicles were obviously capable of such journeys as early as 1920, but travelling these distances on solid tyres with charabanc bodies, even with hoods up, would have made hard going! Such was the satisfaction with the Dennis marque that a further ten were purchased in 1920 though no more of that make entered the fleet until 1933.

Two newspaper cuttings from *The Liverpool Echo*; right dated February 1922 and left March 1922.

At this point in 1920 the LUT fleet stood at 48, being the two 1919 batches of twelve reconditioned ex-WD Dennis chassis with new charabanc bodies (Nos. 1-24), ten more similar from Dennis in 1920 (27-36), seven Fiat 14-seaters (38-44) and three AEC 45/50 hp 33-seaters (45-47). This leaves the two second-hand AECs from Avery & Roberts to take fleet Nos. 25 and 26. Number 37 was believed to be an Orwell non-passenger battery-electric vehicle built by Ransomes, Sims & Jefferies. The Unic does not appear to have been allocated a fleet number and may have been withdrawn prematurely. More AECs appeared later in 1920 (48-59) and a small Daimler CK (60) which survived to be re-bodied by Roe c.1930 and re-numbered 1. Between 1919 and 1923 SLT had reached its maximum fleet size of 89 tramcars and a maximum tram route mileage of 39 miles in 1919. By the standards of the time the company and its subsidiary had reached a considerable size.

The two second-hand AEC covered buses (25 and 26) operated initially the first bus service from Lowton to Haydock. In later years Edwardes reported to WJ Crosland-Taylor that the three AECs (45-47) were "the first new buses we had." AECs 58 and 59 were acquired from Robey of Cadishead; Nos. 61-64 were four more AECs "of a type similar to our own" which were purchased from Liverpool Corporation for £400 each in 1922. They were rebuilt from rear entrance to front entrance thus establishing LUT's general standard of front entrance single-deck bodies which was to remain to the end of single-deck half-cab operation.

During the early 1920s local interest in touring waned so some of the Dennis charabancs were re-bodied as enclosed buses. New bus routes were commenced and as passengers became more plentiful and new services became established the fleet expanded with Bristols in 1923 (65-70) and 1924 (71-72), and the first of many Leylands in 1925 (73-82). The Bristols were part of Harry England's influence (a man who we shall see very shortly as an LUT Board Member) as perhaps was an agreement in 1922 for LUT to act as an agency

A line-up of LUT vehicles in Victoria Square, Bolton opposite the Town Hall, then a regular venue for such gatherings. The date is c.1922. Later in the 1920s Bolton's war memorial was erected to the right of this view. Today, modern shops replace the buildings shown with WH Smith occupying the left of the picture. From the left is one of the Fiat 14-seaters, the solitary Unic KB 344, Fiat TB 165 and some Dennis examples still with their Charlesworth charabanc bodies, the first of which is B 8672. Third from the right is TB 1159.

of the manufacturer for the sale of Bristol commercial vehicles. An order was placed with the English Electric Company of Preston in December 1923 for twelve bus bodies as part of the upgrading of the former charabancs.

With the intention of strengthening the North Wales connection through Tourist Hotels Ltd., it was agreed at the January 1922 meeting to sell two motor buses to the Bangor Blue Motor Company Ltd. in return for shares in that company. The following month it was reported that the two buses had been exchanged for 3,200 one pound shares. The buses were painted into Bangor Blue livery at Atherton before delivery (see page 20).

At the end of 1922, following the death of Mr JM Henderson as reported earlier, Mr Harry England was appointed to fill the vacancy on the Board. A lifelong busman, with two sons who would become well-known in the transport business, he was Managing Director of the Yorkshire (West Riding) Electric Tramways Company Ltd. and its successor the West Riding

Automobile Company Ltd. and a former municipal manager at Bolton and Sunderland. The West Riding company went on to become one of the largest independent bus operators in Britain.

New LUT services continued to be introduced during 1922, including Hindley to Walkden, Leigh to Culcheth and Swinton Church to Hollins Green with some journeys extended to Warrington. In 1923 more new services were Leigh to St. Helens, Walkden to Abram (later extended to Wigan), Peel Green to Warrington and, in August, a daily service to Blackpool. As more buses were required for these services, more Dennis charabancs were re-bodied with closed bus bodies as shown in the photographs on pages 25, 30 and 31. Research continues to try to determine the exact details of these various rebodyings and by which bodybuilders.

Board meetings continued to be held in London at Dashwood House maintaining the routine and location as from January 1906. Also at this time an agency for Hampton cars was taken on, though how successful (or otherwise) is not recorded.

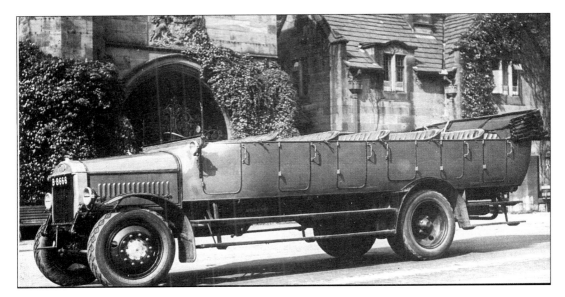

During 1921 coal shortages following strikes in the mines and on the railways had given LUT a flying start with its charabanc business. The following year was to prove more difficult as the economic situation deteriorated, and cut-throat competition from other charabanc operators in the area reduced profit margins.

The party seen opposite with two of the Fiat 14-seat vehicles is standing outside the Glynne Arms at Llangollen. The occasion was a demonstration run for the press; sitting alongside the driver of the first vehicle is believed to be the Chairman, Sir Arthur Stanley; at the rear of the vehicle in his trademark cap is the General Manager, Ned Edwardes. By January 1923 Tourist Hotels had gone into liquidation and LUT had lost its £2000 shareholding, despite having carefully checked out the situation before investing.

As bus services grew the decision was taken to rebuild the charabancs, as above, with enclosed bus saloons on the Dennis chassis. The English Electric Co supplied 12 bodies, the British Commercial Lorry & Engineering Co of Manchester at least 15, whilst LUT may have built some bodies itself since a licence had been obtained to allow the company to build or purchase bodies built to the BMMO design of Midland Red, Birmingham. Strachan & Brown's contribution can be seen on page 30. As technology improved it became possible to fit balloon tyres in place of the solid or NAP units and the presence of Mr Robert Watson, a Dunlop Director, on LUT's board would ensure the availability of the appropriate technical expertise. It could also explain why Lancashire United had an agency for selling Dunlop tyres to private motorists.

LUT possessed sufficient vehicles in the 1920s to carry out large scale private party work. This picture shows 24 of the Dennis charabancs about to embark from Liverpool in 1922. The excursion list for 1923 indicates the extent of the resorts on offer. By this date weekend tours had begun operation.

LUT claimed to have been the first bus operator to have initiated winter services to football matches which created business when the normal coaching season, as advertised in the poster reproduced here, was over. This work continued into the 1960s, notably with a Saturday service from Patricroft to Old Trafford when Manchester United was playing at home, almost replicating the Trafford Park Estates route of 1925. Another claimed 'first', probably drawing on expertise from associates of Arthur Stanley in Dashwood House, was the installation of 'wireless telephony' in one of the bus re-bodied Dennis vehicles during 1922. This was stated to be for the entertainment of the passengers, but also to enable the head office to keep in touch with the driver who used headphones for the purpose. A long aerial consisting of several wires was fitted along the roof to enable the signal to be picked up.

LANCASHIRE UNITED TRAMWAYS LTD.

Motor Coach Excursions

The following Excursions will continue throughout the Season
(Subject to alteration without notice according to circumstances)

			RETURN FARE.
LLANGOLLEN	Regular Daily Service	Coaches will leave 154 Mount Pleasant each day at 10-30 a.m., travelling via Chester, Wrexham and Ruabon. Returning from Llangollen at 6-15 p.m. FARE (including Lunch and Afternoon Tea at PONSONBY ARMS)	14/6
		SATURDAYS	17/-
CHESTER	Regular Daily Service	Coaches leave 154 Mount Pleasant each day at 10-30 a.m., returning from Chester at 8 p.m. (Allowing full day in Chester). RETURN FARE	7/-
BLACKPOOL	Wednesdays and Sundays	Leaving 154 Mount Pleasant at 10-30 a.m., travelling via Ormskirk, Preston and Kirkham. Returning from Blackpool at 6-30 p.m. COACH FARE	12/6
		Or, INCLUDING LUNCH AT IMPERIAL CAFE ..	15/-
DELAMERE FOREST and CHESTER	Wednesdays and Saturdays	Afternoon Circular Tour, leaving 154 Mount Pleasant at 1-30 p.m., via Frodsham, Warrington, through Delamere Forest, TARVIN to Chester. Returning at 7-30 p.m. to Birkenhead, Woodside. Allowing 3 hours in Chester. COACH FARE	7/6
LOGGERHEADS	Saturdays at 1-30 p.m.	Saturday Afternoon Excursion, leaving 154 Mount Pleasant at 1-30 p.m., travelling via Birkenhead, Queen's Ferry and Mold. Returning from Loggerheads at 7-30 p.m. FARE	7/-
	Sundays at 10-30 a.m.	Full Day Excursion on Sunday, leaving Mount Pleasant at 10-30, returning from Loggerheads at 7-30 p.m. FARE	7/-
RUTHIN	Sundays	Leaving 154 Mount Pleasant at 10-30 a.m., travelling via Birkenhead, Queen's Ferry, Mold. Returning from Ruthin at 6-30 p.m. FARE ..	8/6
SOUTHPORT	Sundays	Afternoon Excursion, leaving 154 Mount Pleasant at 2 p.m. Returning from Southport at 8 p.m. RETURN FARE	6/-
EVENING TOUR	Wednesdays Saturdays Sundays	Leaving 154 Mount Pleasant at 7 p.m. for Circular Tour : Childwall, Gateacre, Hunts Cross, Halewood, Hale, Ditton, Cronton, Broad Green. COACH FARE	3/-

WEEK END IN NORTH WALES.

200 MILE TOUR	Saturday	Specially appointed Coaches will leave Birkenhead (Woodside) every Saturday at 2 p.m., travelling via Queen's Ferry, Holywell, Abergele, Conway, Penmaenmawr to LLANFAIRFECHAN (Queen's Hotel). Dinner on arrival and accommodation for the night.	
	Sunday	Breakfast ; thence via Aber, Bethesda, through Nant Ffrancon Pass to Capel Curig, thence via Pen-y-Gwryd and Gwynant Pass to BEDDGELERT (Lunch at Royal Goat Hotel). After Lunch, tour to The Pass of Aberglaslyn. Thence homeward via Capel Curig, Bettws-y-Coed, Pentre Voelas, Corwen, Llangollen (Tea at Ponsonby Arms Hotel), Wrexham, Chester, arriving at Birkenhead (Woodside) at, approximately, 9 p.m. TICKETS (including First Class Hotel Accommodation and Meals)	£3

☞ Tickets for all above Trips are Issued in Advance. All Seats Numbered and Reserved. ☜

Apply to **AVERY & ROBERTS Ltd.** (Liverpool Managers),
Tel. 4393 Royal. **154 Mount Pleasant, LIVERPOOL.**

From 1920 LUT was engaged in the carriage of emigrants in Liverpool. Avery & Roberts Ltd., LUT's agents and managers in Liverpool, arranged with the North Atlantic Passenger Conference, a body which co-ordinated the movements of emigrants, for the transport of these people and their luggage between railway stations, boarding houses, shipping companies' offices and the embarkation dock. This arrangement required a fleet of vehicles which could be rapidly mobilised day and night according to the timing and number of ships due to arrive or depart from Liverpool in any one period of 24 hours. The Dennises, with both charabanc and enclosed bus bodies, and the AEC buses were used on this work. It was suggested in 1920 that LUT was the only company in the country to operate such a service in co-operation with the companies owning ocean-going liners. This business ceased, however, later in the 1920s as larger ships were employed and diverted to Southampton.

A batch of AEC Y-types with 32-seat enclosed bodies by Hora of London was purchased in 1919 by Liverpool Corporation. This example was photographed when new carrying an early form of trade plate. In 1922 four were found to be surplus to requirements and were snapped up by LUT. On arrival they were rebuilt, removing the excessive rear overhang and changing them to the front entrance layout favoured by LUT; they were then numbered 61-64.

LUT saloon buses loading at the Customs Offices at the Pier Head, Liverpool in 1921 in connection with the emigrant traffic. The three vehicles are part of the batch of 14 AEC Y-types purchased in 1920 and said by Ned Edwardes to be "the first new vehicles we'd had." Like the Y-types acquired from Liverpool Corporation in 1922 they are believed to have been converted to front entrance. In the centre is No. 47, TB 1125. The 32-seat bodies were built by a local supplier, the British Commercial Lorry & Engineering Company Ltd. of Manchester.

The annual publication 'Touring by Motor Coach' seen on the facing page lists on its back cover the many services offered to motorists, an interesting instance of services offered to a competing party. Notice that stocks of spare parts are available for Dennis, AEC and Fiat, the principal makes which comprised the LUT fleet at the time. Dunlop tyres were also stocked at Atherton.

Problems continued to be experienced with the tramway operation. As patronage increased, routes became busier and it became desirable to improve both speed and regularity. Many sections of road were too narrow for double tram tracks. Coal mining subsidence continued to affect the track and its maintenance. Considerable capital had been invested in the power station and distribution network and this could not be dispensed with. Even at this early stage (1922) Mr Edwardes had been considering trolleybuses but these vehicles were still of the first generation and were therefore slow and uncomfortable. It was to be 1929 before an Act of Parliament authorised the Company to abandon its tramway, operate a new generation of trolleybuses, and change its name to the South Lancashire Transport Company. A special General Meeting of subscribers was called to obtain the necessary approval of the SLT shareholders.

By 1924 agreements for running motor buses in their areas had been signed with Salford, Warrington, St. Helens and Leigh corporations, and with AA Roberts of Liverpool. Agreement with Bolton Corporation was reported in 1926 but the application to Manchester had still not been approved. Robey was operating as a competitor on the Swinton to Warrington service and his business was purchased for £2,100 at the end of 1924 after some weeks of bargaining.

LUT issued a book entitled 'Touring by Motor Coach' in 1925, providing information on places of interest covering an area from North Wales to Cumberland and East Yorkshire, and announcing tours from Atherton and Liverpool. The remaining charabancs, saloons and 6-seater landaulettes were offered for hire. The latter were Austin cars which were not allocated fleet numbers.

By 1925 diversification was well under way. Private car servicing and repairs were offered day and night at the Howe Bridge, Atherton depot. Agencies were held for Scintilla magnetos and Dunlop tyres as well as for the Bristol commercial vehicles and Hampton cars already mentioned. The Company's involvement with electricity made it especially well-qualified for electrical contracting, and it offered also the installation of private telephones, another spin-off from the Dashwood House companies' connection. Parcels were carried on buses which conductors would deliver to addesses on the route while others could be met and collected at their destinations.

Timetable dated 3rd March 1922 for the inauguration of LUT's route from Hindley to Walkden, from East to West across the Northern limit of operations (see map on p. 29). Note that no layover time is incorporated, and that all the timing points are 'conveniently' though unlikely, exactly ten minutes apart.

Motor Omnibus Services.

NOTICE IS HEREBY GIVEN, that on THURSDAY, MARCH 9th, 1922, A MOTOR OMNIBUS SERVICE will be Inaugurated between :— HINDLEY, WESTHOUGHTON, CHEQUERBENT, LITTLE HULTON and WALKDEN, as follows :—

	FIRST 'BUS.			LAST BUS'.		
	P.M.	P.M.	P.M.	P.M.	P.M.	P.M.
Hindley Council Offices, Cross Street	—	—	1–0	9–0	10–0	11–0
Hart Common Schools	—	—	1–10	9–10	10–10	11–10
Church Street, Westhoughton	—	12–20	1–20	9–20	10–20	11–20
Chequerbent Station	—	12–30	1–30	9–30	10–30	—
Hulton Lane Ends	—	12–40	1–40	9–40	10–40	—
Clegg's Lane, Little Hulton	—	12–50	1–50	9–50	—	—
Walkden Memorial (arrive)	—	1–0	2–0	10–0	—	—
Walkden Memorial (depart)	—	1–0	2–0	10–0	—	—
Clegg's Lane, Little Hulton	—	1–10	2–10	10–10	—	—
Hulton Lane Ends	—	1–20	2–20	10–20	10–40	—
Chequerbent Station	—	1–30	2–30	10–30	10–50	—
Church Street, Westhoughton	12–40	1–40	2–40	10–40	11–0	—
Hart Common Schools	12–50	1–50	2–50	10–50	—	—
Hindley Council Offices, Cross Street	1–0	2–0	3–0	11–0	—	—

and hourly thereafter until last 'Bus. (First Bus columns)
and hourly thereafter until last 'Bus. (Last Bus columns)

Saturday Services will be augmented as required.
Fares and Stages Lists will be exhibited in all Omnibuses.
Detailed Time-table will be published later.

E. H. EDWARDES, General Manager.
Head Offices, Atherton, Lancashire.   3rd March, 1922.

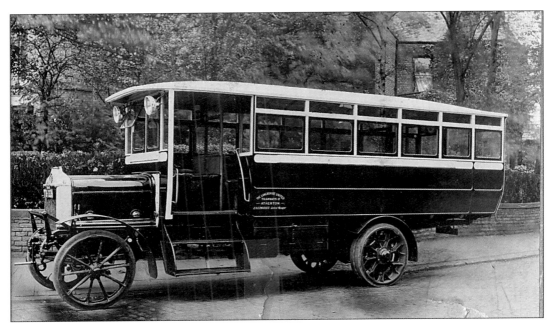

Another view of No. 48, TB 1229, after the rebuilding of the body to front entrance. The legal lettering is at an intermediate stage prior to appearing in an oval shape, a characteristic of LUT and its close neighbour, Leigh Corporation.

The LUT /SLT operating area, below, in 1922. A note at the foot states that services to Warrington connect with Chester, Wrexham and North Wales bus services, no doubt reflecting good relations with Crosville.

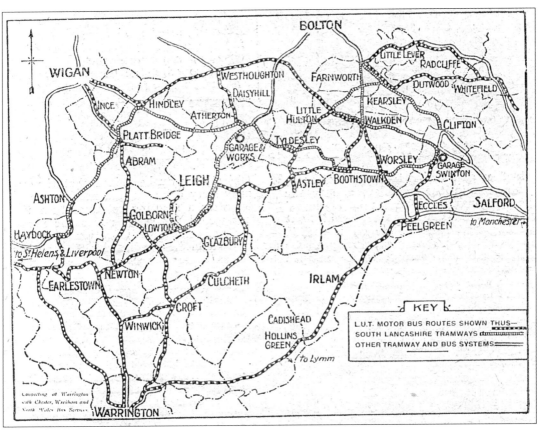

In order to make better use of the Dennis charabancs, it was decided to fit replacement all-weather bodies by Strachan & Brown of London on some of the chassis. The vehicles incorporated a roll-top design enabling the roof to be opened and this, coupled with windows dropping into the body sides, meant that there was nearly as much fresh air as the charabancs they replaced but with the ability to enclose the vehicle when required. The bodymaker's distinctive oval plate can be seen on the nearside front corner.

Note that there is no fleet name other than the legal lettering, which at this time is in parallel line style rather than the oval which was later adopted. The vehicle carries no registration number, nor have the electrics been completed as will be noted by the lack of lamps and profusion of wires. It appears that fleet numbers were not carried, certainly no photographs of vehicles of this period with fleet numbers have so far come to light. (J Lee)

One of the first duties for the new Strachan & Brown vehicles was to carry the victorious Bolton Wanderers football team through the town to celebrate their winning of the FA Cup in May 1923, the famous 'White Horse Cup Final', and the first to be held at Wembley. They found a niche for other special events, including taking a party of delegates from the Tramway & Light Railway Association from Manchester Town Hall to the Chloride battery manufactory at Clifton Junction, but their regular use and the reason they were purchased was to operate from Manchester to Blackpool, which in those days was run as two separate services to Wigan, one via the A57 and the other via the A6. Passengers were transferred to one vehicle which then proceeded to Blackpool. Note that the vehicles were still on solid tyres, ensuring a lively ride!

At the end of 1923 the fleet stood at 70 vehicles, apparently numbered 1-70.

In 1923 a further six Strachan & Brown bodies were purchased but these were conventional buses fitted to Bristol 4-ton chassis as seen in the advertisement below, and carrying fleet numbers 65-70. Number 67 became the SLT tower wagon in later life, lasting until 1958 when the trolleybuses finished and the overhead wiring was removed. It was one of so many vehicles scrapped just before the preservation movement really got under way. *(GLC)*

The growth of the industrial zone within Trafford Park, in the area bounded by the recently-opened Manchester Ship Canal, soon attracted many large companies including Westinghouse (later British Westinghouse and later still Metropolitan-Vickers) thus creating many thousands of jobs. The area was served by Manchester and Salford Corporation electric tramcars, and the Trafford Park Estates Company had also operated its own gas-powered tramcars. By the 1920s TPE was operating a fleet of three AEC S-type buses as seen above, but early in 1925 Lancashire United began negotiations to buy out the operation. LUT's first double-deckers thus arrived in 1925 in the form of these three open-top, open-staircase vehicles, which had been new in 1921, and, together with their running rights, were taken over from Trafford Park Estates Ltd. on 27th June. This company had operated a service between Patricroft and the Trafford Park Hotel to cater for workmen in the burgeoning factories of the Trafford Park industrial estate. After the agreement was concluded LUT began to operate into Trafford Park, thus crossing the previously-observed territorial boundary of the A57 trunk road and the Ship Canal by means of Barton Swing Bridge. The AECs operated a frequent service during the week, and were then offered for private hire at weekends. This route was the precursor of the intensive workmen's services into Trafford Park from Swinton, Eccles, Bolton, Atherton, Leigh and other towns in LUT's operating area. The buses operated from Swinton depot which had been built for the SLT trams in

1906, and later housed LUT buses and SLT trolleybuses. The enormous growth within the Park, in the 20's and 30's and then especially during the war years provided LUT with a huge amount of lucrative additional traffic.

In February 1925 it had been decided to purchase six 36-seat centre-entrance Leyland buses with bodies by Ransomes, Sims, & Jefferies Ltd. of Ipswich, to LUT's design, at a total cost of £9,000 for use on workmen's services. These would be the first Leyland vehicles to enter the fleet and that company, possibly sensing the future potential or perhaps just short of work, offered a discount if LUT would increase the order to ten which it did, the vehicles becoming Nos. 73-82 as seen in the advertisement on the facing page.

These ten, and the English Electric rebodied charabancs, were amongst the first vehicles to carry the 'Lancashire United' name on the bodysides, in the traditional form which continued until the end of the Company's existence; previously the charabancs and buses appear only to have carried the statutory 'legal lettering' with neither fleetname nor number visible. In May 1925 the General Manager reported that he had been approached by the Crosville Motor Co. Ltd. of Chester with a view to amalgamation. By July the Board had resolved after negotiations that nothing further be done.

Years later, another General Manager, Robert Bailey, stated that this was an outright purchase bid by Crosville for LUT which was duly rejected. It is interesting to speculate on the eventual outcome on the history of road passenger transport in the North West if the proposal had gone ahead!

Distinctive Bodywork.

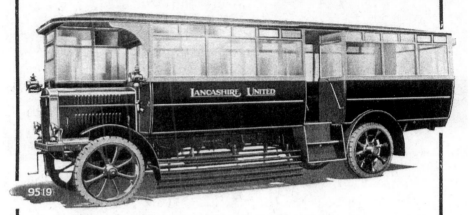

We have exceptional facilities for the production of bodywork of all kinds. Our shops are laid out for dealing with large orders and we have one of the largest stocks in the country of naturally seasoned timber.

Our long experience enables us to offer bus bodies in which the design, materials and workmanship are of the highest class, and the numerous repeat orders we have received afford ample tesim ny to the excellence of our products.

Ransomes

BUS   BODIES

We are at all times ready to submit quotations for all varieties of bodies—double-deckers, saloons, etc., either designed by us or built to customers' own specifications.

RANSOMES, SIMS & JEFFERIES, LTD.,
Orwell Works,   **Ipswich.**

From 1926 Leyland was the main motor bus chassis supplier to LUT until wartime forced a break in 1942. By 1926 the bus fleet had reached 100, running over 21 services and three years later it had grown to 152. A dense network of services had evolved within an area bounded by St Helens in the West, Bolton in the North, Salford (on the Manchester boundary) in the East and Warrington in the South. Most of these were linking services rather than local routes within the towns.

Also in 1926 it was resolved in March, in connection with a major share issue, that the Company name be changed to the Lancashire United Transport and Power Company Ltd to reflect more clearly the wider scope of the business and remove the out-dated tram connotation.

Contrarily, perhaps, a significant new tram service commenced in May 1926 from Walkden to Manchester using Salford lines from a new connection at Swinton Church (St. Peter's). On the bus side the services to Blackpool had been so successful that another six Dennis charabancs were converted to closed buses at a cost of £383 per vehicle at the end of 1926. Also at this time eight second-hand 20-seat Bristol small buses were purchased from Director Harry England's West Riding company at Wakefield.

A major terminus was the Spinning Jenny Street bus station in Leigh opened in 1927. Motor buses moved out to on-street stands in 1933 when SLT trolleybuses commenced the Leigh to Bolton service. It reverted to a motor bus station on the demise of the trolleybuses in 1958. Negotiations had begun in 1926 with Salford Corporation regarding a joint service to Warrington. Agreement was reached in May 1927, the service commencing at Salford Greengate under the arches beneath 'Manchester' Exchange railway station.

Routes in Wigan were opened up to LUT by the purchase in conjunction with Ribble Motor Services Ltd. of Websters Motors bus services in 1927. Negotiations over the price continued for most of the year to try to close the gap between the £15,000 asked by the Webster brothers and the £12,000 offered. The General Manager was eventually authorised to pay the £15,000 and to recover £6,500 from Ribble. The joint purchase was reported in November 1927 and twelve Leyland vehicles of varying ages joined the LUT fleet becoming fleet Nos. 121-128, 35-38, an unusual instance at that time of re-using fleet numbers. Because of the growing bus fleet there was now a need for additional accommodation and it was resolved to convert the existing Hindley (Platt Bridge) car shed. The main Atherton depot was also extended to take 100 buses. Capacities at the other garages at this time were: Platt Bridge 26, Swinton 74, and Liverpool 24.

The General Manager was next authorised to order 20 new buses, ten double- and ten single-deck. These were the first 'modern' buses with low chassis, strengthening what became a long association with Leyland. The buses arrived in 1928 as Leyland-bodied open-staircase TD1s Nos. 129-138 and PLSCs 139-148 with Davidson bodies.

In 1927 ten single-deckers were ordered from the Bristol Tramways & Carriage Co Ltd, reflecting the influence of LUT's Director Harry England, who was of course Managing Director of the West Riding Company, a major user of Bristols. In the event the order for the bodywork was transferred to Davidson of Trafford Park, Manchester when it became apparent that Bristol could not meet the required delivery date. A saving of £50 per body was a further bonus. These vehicles became numbers 111-120 and one is seen opposite in the bodymaker's official photograph. Davidson was using the factory which had previously been used by the Ford Motor Company for the manufacture of Model-T cars but before that it had been used by the British Electric Car Co for tramcar manufacture. When Davidson went into liquidation in 1931 the factory passed to Eastwood & Kenning who continued to build buses there, the name of the new company incorporating the names of two of the former directors of Davidson (Trafford Park) Ltd. *(GMTS)*

Lancashire United was fortunate in not having to purchase many second-hand vehicles throughout the whole of its existence, unless such vehicles came with businesses taken over. The first exception to this was the purchase of eight 20-seat 2-ton Bristols purchased in November 1927 from the West Riding Company, the vehicle below being one of the same type but not one which actually passed to LUT. New in 1924, they became numbers 103-110 but their service life is believed to have been short. *(GHFA)*

TELLING POINTS!

1. Design.
2. Quality.
3. Workmanship.

Total **SATISFACTION.**

Hence, a repeat order for 26 of these Buses.

'Phones :
1098 - 1099
Trafford Park

DAVIDSON
(TRAFFORD PARK) LTD
MANCHESTER

'Grams :
Autobodi,
Manchester

THE LARGEST BODY BUILDERS IN THE NORTH

A somewhat misleading advertisement since the repeat order was for bodies on Leyland chassis ! An unusual feature for LUT was the inclusion of a Davidson-patented sliding front-entrance door, instead of the 'porch' arrangement on which LUT had standardised and to which it soon returned.

LUT was clearly impressed with its Leylands and further orders were placed with the Lancashire company in January 1926. Five Leviathans were ordered at a cost of £1,515 each. They had bodywork by Leyland with an enclosed top deck but open staircase as seen in the photograph alongside. Numbered 86-90 they were joined by a further five, Nos. 98-102, in August of the same year. Totally eclipsed by the Titan TD1 model of 1927 their lives were short and their departure would not have been greatly mourned.

In March of 1926 seven Leyland Lions, as seen below, were ordered at a cost of £1,225.18s each, becoming numbers 91 -97. The Leyland body design was a distinct advance on previous vehicles in the fleet and the model soon became familiar throughout the area with Salford and Leigh Corporations and Ribble Motor Services being amongst other users. The attractive background in this official view is the gatehouse to Worsley New Hall. At this time Leyland was unable to meet the demand for this popular model and many orders were sub-contracted to other manufacturers. The LUT Minutes make no reference to the bodies not being built by Leyland, but it is believed that some or all of the LUT vehicles from this and the later order were sub-contracted to Ransomes, who had built the centre-entrance workmen's buses seen earlier. Leyland, afraid of losing skilled men to its competitors, initially placed such sub-contract work as far away from its Lancashire factory as possible, also using Vickers of Crayford and Short Bros of Rochester, amongst others, thus avoiding potential defections to local bodybuilders Massey, Northern Counties and Santus all of Wigan, and Burlingham in Blackpool for example.

The arrival of the Leyland Titan TD1, with its lowbridge side-gangway bodywork, allowed LUT to put double-deckers onto the Farnworth to Hollins Green service. There were several low bridges throughout LUT's territory, notably those under the LMS railway at Monton, as seen here, and also under the Liverpool to Manchester railway line at Patricroft station. Leyland sent a photographer to record the ability of these vehicles to pass below the low bridges and the General Manager, Ned Edwardes, can just be seen in the front upper-deck window of his new vehicle at Monton. It was also photographed by the trade press as seen below, believed to be at the junction of Folly Lane and Dale's Brow, Swinton. Ten vehicles were ordered in November 1927, becoming numbers 129-138, with a further four in June 1928 being numbered 149-152. Well ahead of contemporary practice, they gave good service, the last not being withdrawn until 1948, and formed a striking contrast with their ungainly and uncomfortable predecessors the high-chassis LG1 Leviathans on solid tyres as seen on the facing page. *(STA, EO coll)*

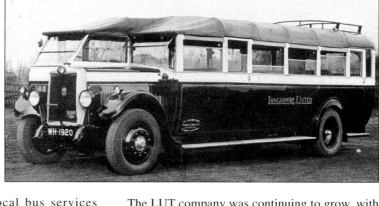

One of the more spectacular Lancashire bus and coach operators was JR Tognarelli of Bolton whose services grew rapidly between 1927 and 1929 when the operation abruptly disappeared from the scene. Tognarelli had commenced a haulage business in 1911, turning to passenger services in 1919 when he offered charabanc excursions. Local bus services commenced after the General Strike in 1926, and a bus service of 30-minute frequency between Bolton and Manchester began in May 1927. A policy of low fares, backed financially by Tognarelli's other interests including a restaurant, gradually stimulated the traffic but provoked keener competition on the part of the railway companies and the municipal bus operators, Bolton, Manchester and Salford. In conjunction with the corporations, LUT ran a competing express service between Bolton and Manchester, providing the vehicles until such time as the corporations could participate. From the end of 1928 to December 1929 Tognarelli also operated a luxury express coach service between Bolton and London. This astutely run organisation, with its ambitious plans and modern, high quality fleet, came to an abrupt end on 9th December 1929 when health and the level of competition, largely provided by LUT vehicles, led the Tognarelli company to sell the local bus services and vehicles to the major operators, and to dispose of the haulage interests. Of the 23 modern vehicles in the sale, Bolton took two, Manchester six, Oldham two, Salford six and LUT seven.

The LUT company was continuing to grow, with more vehicles operating an ever-increasing number of services. Management remained in the hands of the familiar team, except that in 1925 William Watson replaced Robert Watson as a Director. Thus by 1928 the other Directors were the Hon. Sir Arthur Stanley (Chairman), Alfred Adam, John Soame Austen and Harry England. EH Edwardes was General Manager; J Alldred, Traffic Superintendent; WJM Wilson, Rolling Stock Engineer; and Jacob R Holt, Secretary.

The Leyland TS2 Tiger with Burlingham roll-top canvas-roofed body taken over from Tognarelli, numbered 125 by LUT, seen above, represented one of the Leyland types not otherwise represented in the fleet. Six months old at the time of takeover it was one of five vehicles new in that year to the Bolton operator. It was rebodied by Roe in 1933 and remained in the fleet until 1951; the other six vehicles involved were withdrawn within two years.

Two Leyland Tigers pictured below in 1929 while still with the Tognarelli fleet. The saloon coach, WH 1299, carries a Harrington body and was used on the London-Manchester-Bolton-Glasgow service. It joined the Bolton Corporation fleet on the joint takeover. Behind is a sister vehicle to WH 1920, WH 1922, also with a Burlingham canvas-roofed body; it was allocated to the Salford fleet.

In October 1928 a significant extension to the Atherton bus depot had been opened by the Chairman's elder brother, the 17th Earl of Derby. At the same time the General Manager took the opportunity to put on show inside the new building the ten new Leyland Titan double-deckers which must have made a striking contrast with the earlier double-deckers in the fleet. The steady increase in the size of the fleet required further depot accommodation and the complex was gradually extended in the Leigh direction. This photograph, believed to date from 1932, shows a change in design whereby the single, wider, doorway gave access to a very much larger depot space within.

It was also necessary to make considerable alterations inside the original tram depot across the road, in preparation for the forthcoming changeover to trolleybuses. SLT's trolleybuses, initially Guy BTX models, would use this building which, as can be seen, was a typical tram shed with many upright steel stanchions. The restricted space and the fact that the trolleybuses were not equipped with traction batteries (meaning that they could not be manoeuvred away from the wires) necessitated some clever engineering solutions as will be seen on page 54, but here the advance work to create inspection pits is in hand with trams in the background.

Mr Edwardes had considered trolleybuses as early as 1922 but little development had taken place following the early examples.   By 1929 a new generation was available.   Having visited Charles H Roe's factory in Leeds and seen such vehicles he ordered a batch of ten Guy BTX 3-axle trolleybuses with Roe double-deck lowbridge bodies seating 54.   The association between the two companies was to be a long-standing and successful one.   The bodywork shows clear influence of the Leyland Titan with its 'piano front', and incorporated the side gangway on the offside of the upper-deck which was subject to a Leyland patent. It would have been necessary for Roe's to make a royalty payment for the use of this aspect of the design.   Received in 1930 the vehicles were numbered 1-10 and replaced the trams on the route between Atherton and Ashton in Makerfield.   The route was inspected on 28th July 1930, the ceremonial opening took place on the 30th July and public service commenced on 3rd August operating from Platt Bridge depot.

Tilt testing facilities were fairly rudimentary in 1930 . . .

. . . as were the vehicles' interior appointments.

The classic Davidson body with its characteristic destination panel introduced a modern semblance to the LUT fleet in 1929. The 32-seat body was built in Trafford Park, an area served by LUT which was to become much more intensive in WW2. Number 173 was one of a batch of 36 Leyland LT1s numbered 153-188, TE 6665-74, 7064-89. Some remained in the fleet until 1948. The three small lights below the destination indicated LUT buses to staff and passengers at night, a feature on half-cab buses which continued into post-war years.

When new, several of the LT1 Lions were used for a scout jamboree excursion to the Peak District as shown here. Number 173 (TE 7074) leads the convoy which apparently ran in numerical order. While passing through Buxton No. 188 was observed to be at the rear suggesting that 16 vehicles took part. AA patrolmen on motorcycles with sidecars led and brought up the rear.

Atherton workshop scene with vehicles undergoing maintenance or repair. From the left: 1927 Bristol B-type No. 115 (TE 1900), 1923 Bristol 4-ton No. 70 (TC 4006) and 1922 AEC YD-type No. 50 (TB 2513). On the right are two of the original Dennis vehicles, now rebuilt with bus bodies and pneumatic tyres, numbered 19, 20 (B 8771,2).

Many and varied private hires were carried out by LUT, as witness the scouts' excursion, and this visit to Aintree racecourse in Liverpool. These pictures show that temporary folding stands were fitted to the roofs of at least three of the Davidson-bodied Leyland LT1s of 1930. Number 190 (TF 1524) is shown above with the stand folded for travelling. Below, at the racecourse, are Nos. 189 (TF 1523) and 193 (TF 1775) with stands erected and spectators aloft. Other vehicles in this interesting period piece are, from left, a coach of Pearsons of Liverpool (Happy Days Motorways) which operated a service between Liverpool and London, a coach belonging to James Bridge (St. Helens) Ltd. (DJ 4447) evidently on hire to Pearsons, LUT's 1920 Daimler CK rebodied with a Roe 20-seat body and re-numbered 1, and two LUT Leyland LT2s bodied by Eastwood & Kenning, successors to Davidson, Nos. 216 (TF 3585) and 220 (TF 3589). Number 216 was converted to an ambulance in 1940, having received a Leyland diesel engine in 1934 at the time the Company began comparative trials between petrol and diesel units. The superiority of the oil engine was soon recognised and from 1936 all vehicles were fitted with such engines from new, further conversions also taking place. *(GLC, above)*

The arrival of 16 single-deck Leyland Lion LT1 vehicles in 1930 marked the entry into the fleet of motorbus bodies from Charles Roe at Leeds. Roe had, of course, supplied the trolleybus bodywork. Numbers 189-196 were bodied by Davidson and 197-205 by Roe, as shown above. One of the Roe vehicles, No. 202, survived to be preserved and now resides at the Lincolnshire Vintage Vehicle Museum, except for occasions when it attends rallies. Note that the oval style of legal lettering can now be clearly seen. The lower illustration shows the vehicle in early preservation days in Lincoln. These petrol-engined single-deckers were among the vehicles withdrawn during the war years, being replaced by utility double-deckers on a one-for-one basis as required by the Ministry of War Transport directive. Licences were required before new vehicles could be obtained, through allocation, and permits for the disposal of old vehicles were also required. Some, however, survived until 1946 including 202 which then went on to give further service in Jersey.

As the services expanded so also did the properties. Branch offices were now at 81 Renshaw Street, Liverpool; Exchange Hotel, Fennel Street, Manchester; garages were located at Howe Bridge, Atherton; Bentley Road, Liverpool; Partington Lane, Swinton and Platt Bridge, Hindley.

LUT also had space at the Coliseum Garage, Lytham Road, Blackpool, later to become the Coliseum coach station, a regular venue for LUT vehicles, especially on the X60 service.

On the initiative of the Manchester General Manager, Henry Mattinson, express services across the city centre were introduced in 1927. The surrounding municipal operators participated and LUT was also included, working on the Bolton to Salford route from May 1927, extended through Manchester to Hyde in 1928. These services had ceased by 1932 due to complaints by the police of traffic congestion in the city centre and claims by the railways of loss of traffic.

If the cross-city services did not endure, the next venture certainly did and lasted until 1973 as far as LUT was concerned. LUT joined Ribble Motor Services Ltd and the North Western Road Car Company Ltd in a service from a site at Lower Mosley Street, Manchester to Blackpool via Bolton or Westhoughton, Chorley and Preston. Only Ribble was licensed by the Corporation to stop in Bolton, therefore LUT and North Western worked the route via Westhoughton using the A6 road. The new bus station at Lower Mosley Street was opened on 27th September 1929, becoming the terminal point for the Blackpool and other long-distance services in which the three operators were involved, together with some services of Manchester Corporation and other operators. When the 1930 Road Traffic Act came into force the following year, all three companies were licensed to pick up in Bolton whereupon most Westhoughton journeys were diverted via Bolton.

LUT's longest route commenced in 1932 when it joined the Limited Stop Pool which worked the service between Liverpool and Newcastle via Manchester and Leeds. From 1934 there was a branch to Middlesbrough with an extension to Redcar in pre-war summers. There were also various short workings. The other participants were Northern General Transport Company Ltd., which commenced the service in 1928, North Western Road Car Company Ltd., West Yorkshire Road Car Company Ltd. and Yorkshire Woollen District Transport Company Ltd. United Automobile Services Ltd. joined the Pool in 1934 when the Middlesbrough service commenced. LUT's lightweight Dennis Arrows were generally used on these Tyne-Tees-Mersey Express routes.

Two Guy Arab double-deckers, numbered 47 and 48, were purchased in 1933, both fitted with Metropolitan-Cammell metal-framed bodywork supplied through the newly-formed MCW organisation. It may be assumed that they were not particularly successful as they were withdrawn in 1938, although it was company policy to write off its vehicles over five years at the time they were purchased. By contrast, the Leyland Titan TD1s put in some fifteen years or more service.

The Arabs were fitted with Gardner 6LW engines and were the 2nd and 3rd chassis of this model to be built. The bus depicted in the advert was a retouched highbridge Invincible demonstrator and appeared before the completely new, oil-engined-only Arab was announced – the first large passenger chassis that did not have a petrol-engined option. Note the wording linking LUT and West Riding, to which we have already referred, through the directorship of Mr England.

Building on the success of its Titan model, Leyland introduced the more powerful TD2 version, seen opposite. LUT took seven of these in 1932, fleet numbers 38-44, and this maker's view shows the first of the batch before leaving Leyland. Note that the open staircase of the earlier models has now been replaced with an enclosed rear platform. The larger tyres are also noteworthy as is the **Lancashire United** cast name on the radiator. The vehicles were neatly lined-out in gold, but the use of such lining was soon cut back on LUT's double-deckers, though less so on the saloons. The first trolleybuses had seen the peak of this embellishment for double-deckers, as shown on pages 40/41. This bus remained in service until 1951.

Dennis Bros Ltd was naturally keen to continue its association with the company, though in fact none of its products had been purchased since 1920. In 1933 it supplied six petrol-engined Arrow single-deckers, seen on page 52, and a single Lance double-decker numbered 240, TF 7277, which was renumbered 125 and then renumbered again as 100.

The bodywork once again came from Metropolitan-Cammell to its newly-introduced patented metal construction but in fact it was a Chiswick design for the London Underground group. Further details can be found in the publisher's history of the Weymann organisation, but it may be noted here that Northern Counties and other bodybuilders also produced this design for other operators, presumably under licence. The rear lower-deck window was a distinctive feature of this body, identifying it as the former LUT No. 100 when it was used as a builders hut after withdrawal in 1945.

The lower view shows the austere design of the upper-deck, typical of the period and by today's standards distinctly claustrophobic. The wooden rail on the top of the leathercloth-covered seats was a standard LUT feature which lasted into post-war years. Note that the bench seats alternate in threes and fours to assist in passenger and conductor circulation. The white enamel ceiling would very quickly become dark brown in those days when thick-twist was the choice of many smokers. During a wet dark journey, with twenty-plus smokers puffing away, the atmosphere had to be seen and tasted to be believed, yet in those unenlightened days it was taken for granted.

Problems with the SLT trams continued. Insufficient revenue was being generated to maintain the track and renew rolling stock from the inter-urban routes with long stretches through sparsely populated areas. Coal mining subsidence still affected the track, many roads were too narrow to introduce double track for improved operation and the old trams were becoming obsolete when compared with the new generataion of motor buses represented by the Leyland Lions, Tigers and Titans coming into the LUT fleet.

The size and importance of LUT did not go unnoticed by the railway companies. Ashton Davies of the LMS visited Atherton in 1931 to discuss the possibility of the railway company becoming involved with the bus company, but the LUT Directors refused to negotiate and the proposal came to nothing. It was in the following year that General Manager EH Edwardes was appointed to the Board as Managing Director.

LUT was involved in two notable takeovers in the 1930s though these brought no vehicles into the fleet. In January 1935 a Blackpool to Oldham route was taken over from M & H Motors Ltd. of Blackpool jointly with Ribble and North Western. Oldham never came into the operating area of LUT and the route was worked by Ribble and Yelloway.

The only LUT vehicles to be seen regularly in Oldham were those participating in the Tyne-Tees-Mersey Express. The coach business of A Christy (Bolton) Ltd. was taken over jointly by Ribble and LUT in 1938 with a route between Bolton and Blackpool. A smaller purchase was the business of William Lees Ltd. of Radcliffe in 1930. Again this brought no vehicles but a Farnworth to Bury service was gained. Thus while only a few small businesses were acquired throughout its history, LUT grew to be Britain's largest independent bus company entirely on its own development without the aid of any railway involvement, control by the BET or Tilling groups, substantial purchases or amalgamations. This is surely a testament to the standard of service provided, the quality of management and the loyalty of staff.

The last SLT tram being driven from Leigh to Atherton depot by Mr EH Edwardes, General Manager, on the night of 16th December 1933. Mr Edwardes is instantly recognisable by his characteristic cap and moustache. On either side of him are Driver H Battersby and Conductor J Gerrard. The tram is said to have carried 92 passengers on this last journey. Number 7 was one of the original Milnes cars of 1902 subsequently fitted with a top cover. The fares collected on this journey were donated to Leigh Infirmary and an inspector can be seen at the left carrying a box for donations.

When the final SLT tram route between Leigh and Bolton was to be replaced, Bolton Corporation agreed to purchase four trolleybuses to be used on this service. The vehicles numbered 48-51, Leyland TTB4 models, were to be housed at Atherton and maintained by SLT. Leyland was quick to send a photographer to record the arrival of the vehicles from Charles Roe as it was the first order for trolleybuses from SLT. Similarly-bodied highbridge vehicles were being supplied by Roe to Doncaster Corporation. The view above shows the specially posed scene outside Lancashire United's head office at Atherton, and it should be noted that the single storey end of the office building later gained a first storey. The man with the bamboo pole, left, reflects the everyday SLT scene, though later some trolleybus operators would use trolley retrievers, which, operating like a motor car inertia-reel seat belt, automatically pulled down the booms in the event of a sudden, unintended, and potentially damaging, dewirement.

Number 48, seen (right) in Bolton very soon after entering service, demonstrates the difference which different types of photographic plate produced; the Leyland man was by this time using panchromatic material which recorded reds as a lighter shade than the orthochromatic used by the local photographer. Note that these modern-looking vehicles are 'dated' by the inclusion of one of LUT's and SLT's more unusual characteristics – the continuing use of metal plate stencil indicators of the type usually associated with tramcars. The first of the Guy trolleybuses had roller blinds as can be seen on number 1 on page 40, but the cost-conscious LUT organisation then specified metal stencils for the destination, and when adopted after 1938, route numerals, for all its new vehicles from c1930 until c1960. Whether these were manufactured in-house or not, is unknown. The clatter when they fell out from under the stairs of a double-decker when being driven in lively fashion, however, gave an added interest to the journey for younger travellers! *(LM, JMBC all)*

As previously mentioned, Dennis Bros of Guildford made a comeback in 1933 when it supplied six Arrows, numbers 234-239, for use on express services. The design of the Roe body and the front end of the chassis were neat and the vehicles looked extremely handsome as can be seen. Note the raised seats towards the rear over the wheel arches thus avoiding the need either to turn the seats through 90° or, alternatively, to remove one seat over each arch on each side of the vehicle.

The following year two similar bodies were supplied on Leyland TS6c chassis, again with petrol engines. The large header tank with two fillers mounted on the bulkhead clearly indicates that these vehicles were fitted with torque converters. In the later view of the same vehicle it will be noted that the large header tank has now been replaced with an Autovac feed unit and the wording **FUEL OIL** indicates that the original petrol engine has been changed. The Autovac Company, whose products graced the bulkhead of many thousands of vehicles throughout the country, was based in Stockport. (JAS)

This rear view of the first of the two Leyland vehicles described opposite clearly shows the raised seating and also the familiar black rectangles within which white lettering gave the vehicle's weight and, at the rear, its seating capacity. The lining out consists of fine gold lining and black beading, the waistrail being the Roe patented teak rail of course. Numbers 241 and 242, like their Dennis compatriots, lasted in passenger service until 1949. Leyland No. 241 was then converted to become a tower wagon for SLT as seen at the foot of the opposite page.

The first trolleybuses operated from Platt Bridge depot to serve the St Helens route, and there was sufficient room for them to run round that depot before entering it from the rear thus avoiding complications in manoeuvring within. When Atherton depot was converted a traverser with turntable was incorporated into the reconstruction enabling the vehicles to be turned through 180° and to move them to whichever road was required. Number 40 of the 1933 delivery of two-axled vehicles is suitably posed. It is likely that Mr Edwardes, by now Managing Director, had seen tramcar traversers in his days with London United. Swinton, like Platt Bridge, had room to allow access from within the rear of the building, thereby avoiding the need for such sophisticated equipment.

The first Leyland trolleybuses, four TTB4s, were actually owned by Bolton Corporation as described on pages 50-51. The next vehicles, supplied in 1937 and 1938, were eight similarly-chassised models with Roe's current body design as shown here. A feature of the lower deck was the long bench seating, a foretaste of things to come. These vehicles included ideas in the chassis design, especially the repositioning of the electric motor, from Mr Edwardes who worked closely with Leyland to obtain what he wanted. They were numbered 52-59 and all lasted until the end of trolleybus operation. *(JAS)*

A brand new tower wagon, seen here on the right, was purchased in 1937 incorporating a hydraulic telescopic ram and fitted to a Leyland Badger TSA5 chassis which, uniquely, was fitted with a torque converter to allow the vehicle to travel smoothly at low speeds whilst the overhead wiring was being inspected. It was ironic that, as seen on page 52, when TJ 5739 took over this task it had been fitted with a conventional gearbox in place of its original torque converter!

Stranger in town! Leyland Motors was able to use LUT's wires for testing its trolleybuses but it was not until 1936 that any vehicles were actually supplied to the company. In the lower facing illustration a single-decker demonstrator has turned onto the A6 heading towards Walkden in 1933. Leyland also photographed it in Worsley, taking advantage of the picturesque scenery.

Although there had been three metal-framed bodies from Metropolitan-Cammell, LUT's standard from 1928 had been the Leyland composite-bodied double-decker. In 1935 the company took ten Leyland metal-framed double-deckers, Nos. 49-58, on TD4 chassis of which one is seen above ready to leave the maker's factory for delivery to Atherton. The body design was to prove troublesome in most fleets, but some of LUT's examples survived until 1956, although how much rebuilding by the manufacturer might have been necessary is not known. One of the batch, No. 53, was rebodied in 1951 by Northern Counties after an accident and survived until 1960 as seen on page 103.

Metropolitan-Cammell secured its first order for single-deckers when it supplied ten metal-framed examples on Leyland TS7 chassis in 1936. Numbered 1-10, they remained in service until 1952-1956.

Leyland arranged to borrow one of the Dennis single-deckers from the 1936 batch, and its photographer went throught the vehicle with a fine tooth comb. It would appear that the wide Roe doorway was the point of interest and Leyland must have been intent on suppying some of its metal-framed single-deck bodies for comparison with the composite Roe-bodied examples which were clearly very popular with LUT. The interior view of the Dennis clearly shows the seating arrangement and stylish luggage racks.

Number 17 was a one-off oil-engined Lancet II, the first bus in the fleet to have an oil engine from new. It was fitted with a Roe special lightweight body, perhaps partly reflecting the heavier weight of the oil engine. It remained unique in the fleet and was withdrawn in 1949.

In 1936 four Leyland TD4 lowbridge double-deckers were delivered, Nos. 59-62, fitted with the new style Leyland body designed by Colin Bailey and which succeeded the previous V-fronted design as supplied on vehicles 49-58. They were diesel engined and remained in service for some thirteen years, with one of the batch being the last double-decker to carry the traditional livery with grey roof.

The three pin-point marker lights, below the destination panel, used to identify LUT's buses can be clearly seen.

The next single-deckers to be delivered were Leyland TS7s, bodied by Roe to the later BEF design, and of the 22 vehicles in question ten were fitted with 32-seat bus bodywork as shown opposite and numbered 18-27. The other twelve, numbered 101-112, were fitted with 30-seat dual-purpose bodywork. Number 23 was converted to a towing vehicle when its passenger days were over and survived until 1964.

Roe's next delivery was on TS8 chassis, being numbered 113-120 with dual-purpose 30-seat bodies as seen above. Number 114 of this batch has been preserved and is seen in the illustration on page one when a previous LUT celebratory event was held at Manchester's Museum of Transport. A further batch numbered 121-132 was delivered in 1939 with similar bodywork.

The stylish paint schemes were also applied to vehicles supplied by Roe to Yorkshire Traction and West Riding, amongst other companies, subtly drawing attention to the close relationship between this Lancashire independent company and Harry England's company and its BET neighbours. Alternative photographic emulsions give an impression of quite different shades of the LUT red. Route numbering has now appeared, with metal stencil plates for destination and number.

There were also 32-seat bus-bodied versions numbered 149-157 and 158-169 using the same body shell, and six of these were rebodied by Plaxton with full-fronted coach bodywork and 35 seats in 1953 as shown on page 87.

In 1938 the first highbridge vehicles since the Leviathans of 1926 arrived. They were again to the elegant Bailey design and one was used as the Leyland hospitality suite for the 1937 Commercial Motor Show. The batch was numbered 67-81 on TD5 chassis and lasted in service until 1958/9. Number 72, CTC 736, is shown before leaving Leyland.

Also in 1938 came Leyland's first single-decker bodies since 1926. Metal-framed and with 32 seats, they were numbered 141-148 and perhaps this was indeed the reason for Leyland borrowing the Dennis to study the body detail arrangements as mentioned earlier. Some of the batch remained in service until 1957 though the first withdrawals had taken place in 1954. There was intense competition between Charles Roe and Homfray Davies of MCW regarding the relative merits of composite and metal-framed bodywork. LUT remained faithful to the teak framing of the Roe body for its single-deckers, but kept its options open by taking both MCW and Leyland double-deckers – but none from Roe. The only double-deckers from Crossgates were to be the trolleybuses, where metal framing was not allowed with vehicles using traction voltage circuitry for the internal lighting.

The MCW organisation supplied ten further vehicles in 1940, Nos. 89-98. These were lowbridge models on TD7 chassis with metal-framed bodywork, but this time had been built in Weymann's Addlestone factory. Below can be seen the intrusion of the side gangway on a lowbridge double-decker, complete with the warning notice on the back of every seat reminding passengers to 'mind their head when leaving their seat'. Like the Leyland lowbridge vehicles supplied earlier these buses had the Clayton heater fitted on the upstairs front bulkhead rather than, as normal, downstairs. Number 90 was converted to a tree lopper and survived for a further five years after the rest of the batch was withdrawn in 1958.

Storm clouds gather – and another war becomes inevitable

Company loyalty was reflected in the fact that there were many instances of two and even three generations of a family working for LUT. On 24th November 1938, Sir Arthur Stanley, Chairman, entertained to a celebration dinner in Leigh 55 employees who had been in the service of the company for over 30 years. Unfortunately, Sir Arthur was unable to attend but sent a special message to those who had joined the Company at the same time as himself in 1900. Mr Edwardes made several interesting points in his speech: when conversion from tramcars to trolleybuses was made the cost was met out of revenue and no additional capital had been raised for the purpose; he thought that LUT was the first bus company to provide holidays with pay for all its employees; and a pension and life assurance scheme had been approved for the Company's employees. In addition to the 55 employees present that night with over 30 years service, there were also 160 men who had served the Company for 25 years. The outcome of this event was the formation of the LUT 30 Club in 1939, the qualification for membership being the attainment of 30 years service. By the 1960s membership was around 250. In December 1965 220 members attended the annual dinner at the Formby Hall, Atherton when the Chairman, Sir Robert Cary Bt., MP, presented gold watches and certificates.

Vehicle design was progressing, although Leyland's first attempt at the production of metal-framed bus bodies from 1934 proved disastrous for that company. Known as the 'vee-front,' this double-deck body suffered from structural problems which resulted in a rebuild programme for all such bodies in 1935/6. LUT purchased ten lowbridge examples of the type on TD4 chassis in 1935 (49-58, TJ 9376-85). The rebuilding was obviously successful since all ten went on to complete a service life of 20 years. Number 53

Six of the unfrozen TD7 chassis were allocated in 1941, five with Leyland lowbridge bodies (250-4, FTB 41-5). Diverted from the Alexander company they incorporated its distinctive destination arrangement as shown in this view of No. 250, below, outside Swinton depot. *(JAS both)*

Twelve 'unfrozen' Leyland TD7 chassis were allocated to LUT in addition to three earlier examples which in 1941 were frustrated export orders; all three carried Leyland highbridge bodies, each with a different destination aperture (Nos. 247-9, ETJ 531-3). They were offered to LUT by Leyland, subject to the necessary MoWT permits being obtained at Atherton, which was duly accomplished. Number 247, seen above, and destined for Johannesburg, arrived in green and cream. It is shown here in its final livery, remaining in service until 1959.

(TJ 9380) was rebodied by Northern Counties in 1951 after an accident and remained in service until 1960. Leyland recruited Colin Bailey from Metropolitan-Cammell in 1935 as Body Shop Manager. He went on to solve the structural problems and to design a successor body which evolved to become by 1937 perhaps the most pleasing design of double-deck body (see profile view p 60). This basic design, with gradual refinements, continued until the cessation of Leyland body manufacture in 1954. LUT purchased batches on TD4, TD5 and TD7 chassis up to 1942. Single-deckers continued to be specified on Leyland Tiger chassis (TS7, TS8, TS11) most

Number 255, FTB 46, seen above in Atherton depot, carried LUT's first body by the Northern Counties Motor & Engineering Company Ltd. of Wigan, presumably using body parts in stock and thus was only partly to Government wartime utility body specification. This, the sixth of the TD7s, was a precursor of things to come; NCME was to become LUT's main supplier of double-deck bodies in post-war years.

The last of the Leyland TD7 'unfrozen' chassis were allocated in 1942, including two with Roe lowbridge bodies (256-7, FTB 745-6) to full utility standard. The distinctive Roe waistrail remains on No. 257 which has, apparently, only one opening window in the near side upper deck. *(JAS both)*

with Roe bodies, both bus and dual-purpose. Two small batches carried Metro-Cammell bodywork (1-10, ATE 801-10) and English Electric bodies (170-174, ETF 521-525), the latter to BET's 'Federation' (BEF) design.

By 1936 LUT and SLT were operating a total of 600 route miles together with extensive motor coach excursions, seasonal express services, the Tyne-Tees-Mersey and the Blackpool routes. Motor buses totalled 176 and there were 51 trolleybuses. Both before and after World War 2 the SLT trolleybus system was used by Leyland Motors for trials of its trolleybus chassis, some fully bodied and some in chassis form.

There were five Directors (max. 12. min. 5); Sir Arthur Stanley (Chairman), Edward Henry Edwardes (Managing Director), John Soame Austen, Harry England and John Hill Watson. Jacob R Holt was Secretary, John Farrimond Traffic Superintendent and WJM Wilson Rolling Stock Engineer. Debenture stock due for redemption in 1936 was replaced by £300,000 of 5½% cum. pref. shares issued in 1934. In 1935 the authorised capital was increased from £500,000 to £600,000 by the creation of 100,000 ordinary shares of £1 each of which 83,330 were issued to the debenture stock holders in consideration of the surrender of deferred debenture stock of the same amount. The share capital thus totalled £600,000 (£576,208 issued) and the debenture stock £300,000 (£250,000 issued). A dividend of 7½% was paid on the ordinary shares for 1936. The Company was, therefore, in good financial health with regular batches of top-of-the-range heavyweight vehicles paid for as delivered. Indeed LUT's substantial bank balance was soon to be an embarrassment, with the prospect of punitive tax on excess profits.

The death of Mr J Ainsworth, Swinton Depot Superintendent, in 1938, caused a series of staff movements. William Edwardes, the son of the Managing Director, moved from Atherton to take charge at Swinton and Alan Roughsedge was

Perimeter seating was introduced on some single-deckers to increase passenger capacity by providing more standing space. The two pictures opposite show 'before' and 'after' as applied to the 1931 Leyland LT2s. Bulbs have been removed from the side window lights and the ceiling lighting has been fitted with shades to direct downwards the limited lighting in an attempt to render the vehicles inconspicuous to enemy aircraft at night.

transferred from Liverpool to Atherton. The Bentley Road depot in Liverpool would soon be in use for a very different purpose, as in October 1940 it was requisitioned by the military. Since it had been used chiefly for private hire work, and such work had by then been discontinued, its loss was actually a bonus by reducing operating costs.

However, whilst the above staff changes were taking place, in February 1939 Fieldsends Coaches was put on the market and LUT investigated the situation, but decided against taking any action.

A standard had by now been established of Leyland chassis with Leyland double-deck bodies and Roe single-deck bodies, but this was to change with the outbreak of World War 2 on 3rd September 1939 as will soon become apparent.

In a sign of forthcoming dangers, a 1930 TD1 (TF 3568) was used for wartime livery experiments and buses began to appear with areas of white around the edges of the mudguards and at the rear of the body. Headlamps were masked with light shining dimly through three narrow slots. Low-powered and sometimes blue bulbs were used for interior lighting to reduce any risk of being seen from aircraft. Driving at night was even more difficult since street lighting was switched off.

The coalition Government soon realised that more buses would be required to carry the increased numbers of workers engaged in the war effort, especially with munitions, engineering and coal mining, all major industries within LUT's territory. New vehicles, built to the Government's utility specification, could be obtained only by licence from the Ministry of Supply, dependent upon the operator being judged to be in need of extra vehicles for war work. As seen, three 'trapped' Leylands arrived in 1941 and others were diverted from the Alexander fleet in Scotland. These buses cost 25-30% more than their pre-war counterparts – inflation had arrived.

LUT now placed an order for 60 buses to be delivered from Leyland after the end of hostilities in order to gain a place in the post-war rota. However, the utility vehicles allocated by the Ministry were to set the scene for the fleet in post-war years.

Guy and Daimler were directed by the Ministry to build double-deck bus chassis during the war. Bedford built single-deck chassis but LUT took none of these, since its requirement was to increase the carrying capacity of the fleet by changing from single- to double-deck vehicles.

Pictured in full wartime grey livery with conductress, 1943 Guy Arab II No. 294, FTD 587 with NCME body, displays the white edging, angular rear dome, masked headlights, limited opening windows and wooden slatted seats. During wartime many buses were painted thus.

Several bodybuilders were involved but these bodies appeared to be randomly allocated with no regard to operators' preferences. Hence LUT was to receive its first modern Guy chassis (apart from the two from 1933, and thus hardly modern) and its first Northern Counties Motor & Engineering Co Ltd. (NCME) body, although these were locally built at Wigan. Based on wartime experience this combination, together with the Gardner engine, also built in LUT territory at Peel Green, was to become the double-deck standard in post-war years up to the cessation of Guy bus manufacture.

In all, 62 utility double-deckers (58 Guys and 4 Daimlers) were allocated to LUT from 1942-5. During 1942 LUT received two bodies by East Lancashire Coachbuilders of Blackburn, though the Board Minutes are clear that the intention from the MoWT was that four bodies from this concern would be allocated to LUT. Mounted on Leyland TD5 chassis (FTB 749-50, 260-1) they were destined to remain the only examples from that company ever to join the fleet, yet they remained in service for 18 years.

Although several land mines fell near its depots, causing minor damage to the roofs of buildings, and one bringing down 1,200 yards of overhead wiring in Atherton, LUT survived the war years with little serious loss or damage. One casualty was Leyland TD5 No. 75 (CTC 739) which received bomb blast damage in 1942. Almost

every window was blown in and the bodywork was severely punctured. After repair it went on to see another 17 years service.

Batches of Guy Arabs were delivered in 1943, 1944 and 1945, the only other buses received during these years being four Daimler CWG5s in 1943, three with bodies by Brush (277-9, FTD 182, 181, 183) and one with NCME body (286, FTD 188). The Daimlers were disposed of after 13 years while most of the Guys went on to give another five years service. Another Guy (316, FTE 337) was rebodied by LUT in 1957 and is thought to be the only instance of an LUT-built body since the charabanc era of the 1920s.

Significantly, SLT was allocated six utility trolleybuses to supplement the coal miners' services to the many collieries close to the trolleybus routes. These were Nos. 60-63, (FTD 452-5) in 1943 and Nos. 64-65 (FTE 152-3) in 1944, 2-axle Sunbeam/Karrier Ws with Weymann highbridge bodies. Fitted with upholstered seats by SLT (probably from withdrawn single-deckers) rather than the wooden slatted ones then obligatory they remained in the fleet until closure in 1958.

Even the large allocation of 'unfrozen' and utility buses and the six trolleybuses proved insufficient for the vastly increased worker traffic due to the many factories and coal mines in the LUT/SLT operating area. Almost one hundred buses were hired from other operators including

LUT was always interesting because of the great variety in its vehicles, but No. 309 (FTE 330) was unique in the fleet. The 1944 Guy Arab II was rebodied by Samlesbury of Blackburn after an accident in 1950. The original body was by Massey, the batch being Nos. 308-13. In the days before fleet lists were available it was necessary to see every single vehicle in the fleet to be sure as to just exactly what it was. And even then were still traps for the unwary, like the two Brush-bodied Daimler CWG5 utilities registered in reverse order to their fleet numbers 277 and 278 out of the batch of three, Nos. 277-9.

Number 315, FTE 336, was one of the pair 314-5 which brought body builder Strachan, or more accurately its successors, back into to the fleet; the last examples had been supplied in the 'twenties. The body retains its original destination display, with metal number stencils and normal roller blind for the destination. Note the Alexander arrangement on the unfrozen Leyland behind the Guy. The location is in Trafford Park by the railway lines which ran alongside the roads and into the factories. This was a feature of Britain's earliest industrial estate from the beginning of the twentieth century and was an early example of road/rail interchange.

Number 302, FTE 35 was one of a batch of Weymann-bodied Guy Arab IIs (298-307, FTE 31-40) received in 1944, but seen here some 14 years later at the top of Moorside Road returning to Eccles. It shows the LUT standard indicator display which was fitted throughout the double-deckers in the fleet when they underwent major overhaul, eliminating in some cases the metal stencils used for route numbers and/or destinations. (JAS all)

SLT received six utility Weymann-bodied Sunbeam/Karrier W trolleybuses since it serviced many coal mines which were essential for the war effort. Four arrived in 1943 (60-63, FTD 452-5) and two in 1944 (64-65, FTE 152-3).

Manchester, Bolton and Oldham corporations and the Ribble company. Some came from as far afield as Eastbourne and London. Thirteen AEC Regents from its ST class, new in 1931, were provided by London Transport between 1942 and 1944, many staying for the full two years. They were powered by petrol engines and carried LGOC's Chiswick-built bodies apart from one each of Short and Strachan manufacture, all seating 49.

Again, and no doubt due to the scarcity of photographic film in wartime, no photographs have appeared of LUT buses operating on producer gas. In order to conserve petrol the Government decreed in 1942 that 10% of fleets should be converted by July 1943. This entailed an anthracite-burning trailer being towed, the gas so produced being piped to the engine and fed through the carburettor. This method was highly inefficient: engine power was severely reduced, starting was difficult and hill climbing uncertain. Furthermore, the trailer had to be prepared and petrol had to be introduced into the system to assist starting. Thirty trailers would have been required to convert 10% of the fleet but by the target date less than half had been delivered and only five were in use with Leyland TD1 and TD2 double-deckers. It is thought that few, if any, more were used.

While many petrol-engined single-deckers were withdrawn during the war years, and replaced with utility double-deckers, no TD1 or TD2 vehicles were withdrawn until 1948. Some had been fitted with diesel engines and continued into the early 1950s. The last open-staircase buses (126-8, TF 339-41) remained in service until 1949.

A major loss to LUT was the death of Board Member JS Austen, aged 80, in January 1942. He had masterminded the Company's finances since becoming a Director in 1906 – and maybe before – and maintained a very positive link with the BET

organisation since he was, as previously explained, its Chairman until his death. Board meetings had been held in his office in Dashwood House in the City of London until February 1935, then at the Treasurer's House, St Thomas's Hospital, London, and in Marlborough immediately after the London blitz of 1941, though Mr Austen had continued to attend LUT Board meetings until June 1940. The Company Minute Books from July 1943 have not yet been found – any suggestions as to their whereabouts would be welcomed – but clearly the BET 'connection' had gone. HC Drayton, Austen's number two, had been involved in LUT's affairs when his boss had been 'otherwise engaged', but this situation does not appear to have continued after 1942. That was, of course, the year that Tilling and BET adjusted their shareholdings and spheres of company influence, resulting in North Western and Crosville 'changing camps' as it were.

Sir Joseph Nall MP, a man with business interests – including road haulage – in Manchester, was appointed to take Mr Austen's place on the Board on 11th March 1942. He would become Chairman in 1955, remaining as such until 1958.

Harry England died in 1945, having apparently relinquished his Directorship sometime earlier.

Thus by 1944 there were only four Directors: Sir Arthur Stanley (Chairman), EH Edwardes (Managing Director), Col. Sir Joseph Nall and JH. Watson. Jacob R Holt remained Secretary.

.

The last of the big run of lowbridge utilities, No. 297, FTD 590, was a Guy Arab II received in 1943 and registered singly. Seen here in Farnworth King Street it was the last Roe double-decker to join the fleet, although Roe single-deckers and coaches continued to be ordered until 1955.

Number 311, FTE 332, one of the Massey-bodied batch of Guy Arab IIs of 1944 (308-13, FTE 329-34) seen in Walkden around 1958 with its original body, but now refurbished with remounted windows including top sliders, and revised destination panel. *(JAS both)*

Peace, problems, delays and shortages

World War Two ended on 15th August 1945 with the defeat of Japanese forces and LUT's final 'utility' bodies, now to a relaxed specification, were received at the beginning of 1946. In fact, the NCME bodies on Guy Arab II chassis were almost to normal peacetime standards (320-3, FTJ 936-9). When choice was again possible, LUT chose Leylands in 1946, Dennises in 1947 and both Leylands and Dennises in 1948. Single-deck bodies were by Roe and double-deck bodies by Leyland and Weymann. Guy Arab IIIs appeared in 1949, both single-deck and double-deck, with a batch of the latter bodied by NCME (385-94, KTE 621-30). These handsome bodies were built to LUT's specification whereas earlier post-war bodies had been the builders' standard products. They featured superior seating with greater legroom and air changing equipment on the top deck. They were employed on long-distance routes such as the X60/X70 Blackpool services and the No. 10, Salford to Warrington.

The Rt. Hon. Sir Arthur Stanley died on 4th November 1947 having been Chairman for 45 years and Mr EH Edwardes was appointed to succeed him. On 1st April 1948 the electricity supply industry was nationalised by the Labour Government. This entailed the generating station being operated on behalf of the Central Electricity Authority and power having to be purchased from the North Western Electricity Board, the new distributing authority. Consequently, the Company name was changed on 25th November 1948 to Lancashire United Transport Ltd., its final form.

SLT's last trolleybuses joined the fleet in 1948 in the form of three-axle Karrier MS2s with Weymann 64-seat bodies (66-71, HTD 863-8). These majestic vehicles were destined for a short life, being withdrawn on closure of the system on 31st August 1958.

In 1948 the nationalised British Transport Commission endeavoured to acquire the Company but it was decided to await the introduction of an area passenger transport scheme as envisaged in the 1947 Transport Act. In the event such a scheme was not proposed for South Lancashire. It was to be another Transport Act, that of 1968, which would have drastic consequences for LUT.

Number 321 was part of a batch of four (Nos. 320-3, FTJ 936-9) which were built to the 'relaxed' utility specification in 1945 and registered at the beginning of 1946. The bus is on route 11 between Pendlebury and Eccles and the location is Folly Brook, Monton. *(JAS)*

The first true peacetime deliveries came from Leyland, and during 1946 twelve PD1 double-deckers and five PS1 single-deckers were received. At this time home market customers had to wait their turn, particularly for single-deckers from Leyland. Numbers 324-7, were bodied by Weymann with their standard and attractive highbridge bodywork as above, whilst the other eight, Nos. 328-35, carried Leyland's equally attractive equivalent. Note that in both cases the radiator surrounds are painted, chromium for plating being unavailable at that time due to post-war shortages. They continued the numbering system which had reached 246 in 1934, and then after 1941 climbed to 323 with unfrozen, utility and relaxed-utility vehicles, whilst the single-deckers, Nos.202-206, were starting to fill gaps created by older vehicles which had been withdrawn. There would be no more vehicles from Leyland until 1948. *(JAS above)*

Dennis vehicles returned to the fleet in 1947 for the first time since the Lancet II of 1936 and all the deliveries that year came from the Guildford factory. Numbers 193-201 were Lance models with Weymann lowbridge bodywork, being withdrawn between 1961 and 1965. The two photographs here show the continuation of the pre-war livery style with black horizontal beading, pale cream relief, and grey roof contrasting with the bright red. Gold lining has now been discontinued on double-deckers. Sharp-eyed readers will notice that no fuel filler access can be seen on either photograph; it must be assumed that either Dennis or LUT was changing sides at this time. LUT's preference was for offside fillers but clearly at this time they could be on either side. Diesel engined vehicles were, however, clearly marked FUEL OIL on the panels by the access point once oil and petrol engined vehicles were operating in the fleet.

Three views showing the standard LUT single-decker of the early post-war period. Roe was back as principal supplier of saloons, both as buses and in dual-purpose form, both based on the BEF design bodyshell. Note that by the time of these photographs, after the first repaints, gold lining had been discontinued.

In this view Leyland PS1 No. 202 is about to work back to Manchester from Liverpool. *(KWS)*

The Dennis Lancets, numbered between 336 and 355, were in three batches. The first ten were to dual-purpose specification whereas the balance was intended for bus work. The final five were fitted with Dennis O6 engines and were withdrawn in 1955; the others, all with Gardner 5LW engines, lasted until 1959. Number 348, one of the Gardner-engined examples, is seen in Eccles bus station ready to work the 87 service over Barton Swing Bridge into Trafford Park. *(JAS)*

In this view in Liverpool's bus station, Guy Arab III No. 186 reveals that the crew have cunningly set the blind to MEL (the usual abbreviation for Magnesium Elektron Ltd of Clifton Junction, a workmen's service), to confuse any would-be passengers and deter them from boarding before departure time. One of six, it marked the Guy company's entry into the post-war fleet with its first peacetime deliveries since 1933, undoubtedly following the success of the huge intake of utility vehicles. *(KWS)*

At this point during the Christmas blitz of 1940, Salford No. 68, a 1938 Titan, received a direct hit from a bomb which pierced the railway tracks above, and was totally destroyed.

Fifty-five new vehicles joined the fleet in 1949, Guy, Leyland and Dennis single-deckers and Guy and Dennis double-deckers. The fleet continued to grow throughout the 1950s, the total number of motor buses in service being 346 in 1949, 408 in 1954 and 435 in 1958 (299 d/d, 103 s/d and 33 coaches). By the end of 1958 Guy had come to the forefront with 220 chassis, in addition to which there were 107 Leyland, 39 Dennis, 24 Daimler, 40 Atkinson and 5 Foden, all of which, except for the Leylands, were powered by Gardner engines.

At the same date bodywork showed an even greater variety of makes with 157 NCME, 98 Roe, 56 Weymann, 50 Met-Cam, 42 Leyland, 10 Duple, 6 Plaxton, 6 Strachan, 5 Massey, 2 East Lancs., 2 Willowbrook and 1 Samlesbury. In a far from standardised fleet, the prominence of Guy and NCME had now been established.

LUT was said to operate more workmen's services than any other British bus operator. About 92 services covered 44 different destinations serving 12 collieries and 32 factories including L Gardner & Sons Ltd., LUT's favoured engine supplier, and the Trafford Park industrial estate which required 50 buses daily. The 76 ordinary services operated in 1958 also carried heavy industrial traffic, though with shift work

widespread in the area there was some levelling out of peak travel periods.

Nineteen-fifty saw the first major change in livery since the early 1920s. The original charabancs had been painted in torpedo grey before the change to red and white (or cream) which became the standard scheme. The new livery comprised all-over red with black mudguards. The following year a cream band was added above the lower deck windows and this remained the main livery until the end. Ten Dennis Lance double-deckers with Weymann bodies delivered in 1949 were the last lowbridge vehicles purchased (415-24, LTB 261-70). A departure in 1951 was the purchase of five Fodens with NCME double-deck bodies (447-51, NTC 243-7).

LUT's first true coaches arrived in 1951 in the shape of 10 Guy Arab IIIs with Roe 35-seat bodies as illustrated on the front cover (437-46, MTJ 81-90). It is interesting to note that these handsome half-cab coaches were delivered at a time when underfloor-engined vehicles were becoming available. Received in the red and black livery, they were soon repainted into a red and predominantly cream colour scheme. All were withdrawn in 1964/5 but No. 440 was saved for preservation, later being taken into Heritage work, and still occasionally appears on the rally scene.

Lancashire United's vehicles could be found in bus stations across the north west and as far away as Leeds and Middlesbrough. The prize for the least attractive would without doubt have gone to Salford's Greengate Arches, seen opposite, a dark, damp and dismal place in which to have to wait for a bus, particularly at night. One of the 1935 delivery of TD4s is seen here waiting to take its share of the homeward bound evening rush-hour traffic. Bolton had a selection of termini but Howell Croft had the added interest of trolleybuses working the service to Leigh. Above, one of the post-war Weymann-bodied Karriers is followed by a Roe-bodied Leyland. In the views right and below we see a Leyland lowbridge-bodied PD1A about to leave Liverpool, heading back to Manchester's Lower Mosley Street bus station and clearly getting a good send-off from well-wishers for a party amongst the passengers somewhere on board. *(JAS above, KWS right and below)*

Guy's first post-war double-deckers arrived in 1949 in the form of ten Arab III models with standard Weymann lowbridge bodywork as seen on the facing page and numbered 375-84. Number 382 is seen at Swinton Church in the later (post-1952) livery. The next ten, Nos. 385-94 carried Northern Counties bodywork of that manufacturer's then current style with standee windows and the prominent curved top-deck domes. These vehicles were fitted to a high standard, with seating for just 51 passengers giving more leg room and making them suitable for longer distance use on services such as the X60 and X70 to Blackpool. Number 389 was photographed before the application of the fleetname transfer, and No. 391 after completion. Note the large, ornate fleet numerals which were soon replaced with a similar but smaller version as shown on page 79 and elsewhere. The front dome treatment harks back to pre-war styling. *(JAS, facing)*

During 1949 a further fifteen Dennis chassis arrived, five carrying Weymann single-deck bus bodywork as seen above, and numbered 410-14 of which 414 is seen in the forecourt of Swinton depot on the occasion of an Omnibus Society visit in June 1956. The party was taken through the depot on the trolleybus, and those on the upper-deck were surprised to see a huge pile of discarded triple union flags on their little metal frames – left over from the 1953 Coronation when all vehicles carried them and by then dumped on top of an internal office roof! Ten double-deckers, numbered 415-424 carried the familiar Weymann lowbridge double-deck bodywork. The single-

deckers had Gardner 5LW engines and lasted until 1960, the influx of underfloor-engined vehicles with 44 seats making them less economical to operate; the 53-seat 6LW engined double-deckers lasted until 1965. *(JAS)*

One of the Weymann Dennis Lances shows the post-1952 colour scheme. The red with cream band livery may be more practical, and cheaper to apply, but it deprives the vehicle of the elegance of the earlier batch as shown on page 72. A coat of paint on the radiator also mars the appearance. Plain gold numerals have now replaced the former outlined and shaded ones. *(AEJ)*

A surprise delivery in 1951 was a batch of five Foden PVD6G double-deckers carrying Northern Counties bodywork but this time with 57 seats for normal bus work. The 6G of the chassis designation indicated that the vehicles were fitted with Gardner 6LW engines and the batch lasted in service until 1966. Also delivered in that year were ten Guy Arab IV models with Weymann highbridge bodywork also seating 57 and which also lasted until 1966. Foden No. 447 is seen above at the rear of Salford's Greengate Arches waiting to move forward and join the line of vehicles queueing to pick up passengers, whilst below Guy 460 awaits its turn of duty on the joint service number 8 to Bolton in Salford's Victoria bus station, just across the main road from Greengate. Behind the vehicle is the roadway leading up to the now-closed Manchester Exchange railway station whilst to the right can be seen the base of the tower of Manchester Cathedral. *(GHFA, both)*

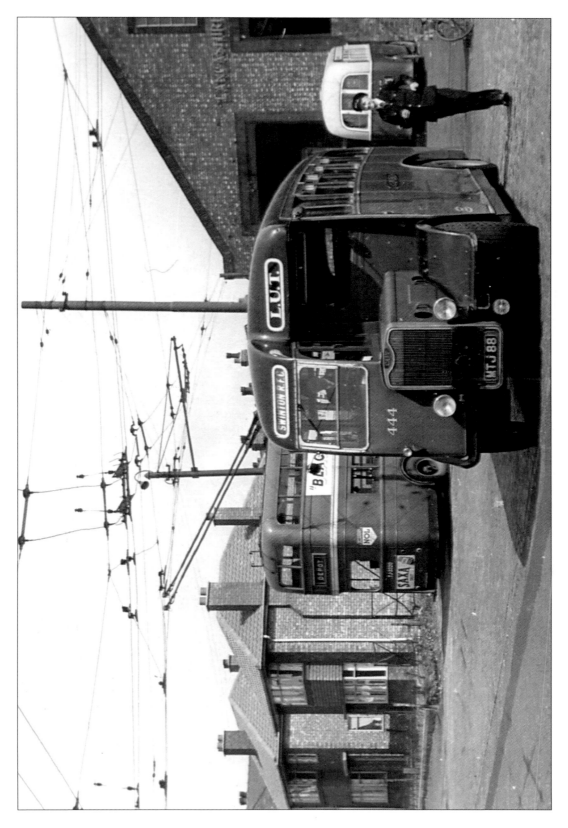

LUT's first true coaches since the 'twenties were delivered in 1951, comprising a batch of ten Guy Arab III vehicles with Roe half-canopy coachwork as seen above and on the facing page. Carrying numbers 437-446 they could be found on a variety of duties including excursions and private hire, among more mundane trips on workmen's services! On the facing page No. 444 leaves Swinton depot on a private hire for Swinton Rugby Club, passing a trolleybus heading into the depot and one of the Roe saloons awaiting its next duty. The black and red livery soon gave way to the red and cream seen on 445 on an excursion into the Peak District in the illustration above.

The change of livery after the brief flirtation with all-red and grey roofs gave way to a lighter shade of red of a more orange hue, with a cream waistband as seen below. Those with long memories may remember the introduction of thixotropic, or non-drip, paints of which Jellipex was a pioneer. LUT took to this and for many years, if not until the end of its existence, that was what its painters used. Whilst the vehicles undoubtedly look smart the loss of the off-white with grey roof was regretted by many. Coincidentally, near-neighbour North Western was at the same time making a very similar change to its single-deck livery as economy measures became necessary to combat ever-increasing operational costs. *(JAS, all)*

In 1952 Guy supplied a further seven chassis, but of the then newly-introduced Arab UF model where the horizontal Gardner engine was sited amidships under the floor. Roe supplied the rather severe-looking coachwork for these, which became Nos. 472-478, but their appearance was greatly enhanced when the revised colour scheme was applied to them. Number 477 is seen parked up awaiting the return of rugby fans near Swinton's ground, a Mecca for seeing the LUT fleet on Saturday afternoons in the 'fifties, while the youngster behind the vehicle seems to be wondering where the engine is as the vehicle has no radiator! Compatriot No. 476 is seen in the familiar location at Blackpool Coliseum Coach Station on a duty more in keeping with its specification. Monday morning could well see it on its way to Metro-Vickers in Trafford Park on a workmen's service since vehicle utilisation at LUT was second to none! *(JAS, both)*

Underfloor-engined Guy coaches arrived the following year, again with Roe bodies originally in red and black and later repainted into cream and red. Also in 1952 a new make was introduced into the fleet. Heavy goods vehicle manufacturer Atkinson of Walton le Dale, Preston ventured briefly into the passenger vehicle market and not without success. This was due in some measure to the desirable Gardner engine, employed here in its horizontal five cylinder form. The Alpha single-deck chassis purchased by LUT carried NCME bodies in two configurations: 44-seat front entrance (6) and 34-seat centre entrance (4). The latter were high-capacity standee vehicles with a large central standing area intended for short heavily trafficked duties such as some workmen's peak hour services. More Atkinsons arrived in 1953, 54 and 55 (10 in each year). The 1955 batch carried Roe bodies furnished to a high standard and painted predominantly cream with red. The legal lettering proclaimed them to be owned by SLT. They proved durable and successful but the manufacturer was unable to secure larger orders from BET – its main target – and production virtually ceased after 1955.

Notable in 1954 was a batch of six Weymann-bodied semi-coaches on Guy UF chassis (516-21, STF 201-6). These outstanding vehicles were used mostly on the Tyne Tees Mersey routes and ran up a great mileage during their 15 years service.

The year 1955 was a significant one in the history of LUT. Mr EH Edwardes, employed since 1902, General Manager since 1910, Managing Director since 1932 and Chairman since 1947, retired in April at the age of 80. Sadly, he died later in the year, on 5th November.

He was replaced by a widely experienced man, Cyril Charles Oakham, who had served in the manufacturing industry with AEC and trolleybus builder BUT, and on the operating side with London Transport, and Manchester Corporation where he had been Chief Engineer. Mr Oakham had also worked at Newcastle Corporation and so all his operating employers had run trolleybuses. Mr Edwardes was succeeded as Chairman by Sir Joseph Nall, a prominent Lancashire road haulage operator and businessman who was also an MP.

Mr Oakham's influence was evident in 1956 by the arrival of 24 Gardner-engined Daimler CVG5 double-deckers with Metro-Cammell bodies seating 61 (570-93, YTD 871-94). They possessed a very Manchester-like appearance with three-part destination display and similar livery of red with cream band. More Guy Arab IV double-deckers with NCME bodies followed later in 1956, and in most years until 1967 when production of Guy PSVs diminished, finally ceasing in 1969. Two batches of five Duple-bodied coaches on Leyland Leopard chassis arrived in 1957 and 1958, bringing a new body make into the fleet.

The Atkinsons transformed the LUT single-deck fleet, none more so than the centre-door examples, popular with parties of anglers as the fishing gear could be easily accommodated in the standing area. The previous centre-entrance buses, Leyland SG11s, are seen on page 33.

Later in 1952 came the first underfloor-engined buses, as opposed to the coaches seen on page 82, Nos. 479-484 with Northern Counties 44-seat front-entrance bodywork on the Atkinson Alpha chassis manufactured at Walton le Dale near Preston in Lancashire. North Western had been actively encouraging that company to produce an alternative to the Leyland Royal Tiger and Tiger Cub models to try to break Leyland's dominant grip on the market, and when the model became available Lancashire United became a ready convert since the vehicles were fitted with Gardner engines. Number 484 is seen on a private hire soon after delivery. The driver's 'cab' had a fixed internal partition and his access was from the outside, as can be seen by the position of the door in this view. (GLC)

Number 496, RTC 687, is one of the two Willowbrook bodied Alphas of 1953 with a capacity of 44, being very similar in external appearance to the first NCME design. Gardner developed horizontal versions of its LW series engines for underfloor engined chassis in four, five and six cylinder forms and the 5HLW version was used in these LUT examples. *(JAS)*

The ten Alphas for 1954 carried Roe 44-seat bodies . Number 530, TTD 299, is shown below when new at the Roe factory in Leeds. Note the front dash panel incorporates a representation of the Roe patented teak waistrail.

Roe-bodied Alpha No. 525, TTD 294 is emerging from under the low railway bridge at Clifton Junction. This industrial and railway background illustrates one of the many diverse kinds of topography which LUT served within its operating area. Chloride batteries, Pilkington Tiles and Magnesium Elektron were among the many companies LUT served here. The railway line from Patricroft was severed when the infamous Black Harry tunnel collapsed in 1952. *(JAS)*

Many operators indulged in the rebuilding and rebodying of older vehicles in the austerity years following World War Two. In many instances double-deckers could give further service when replacement bodywork was fitted to reconditioned chassis, whilst in other cases it was felt necessary to update half-cab coaches on the advent of underfloor engined vehicles with full fronts. LUT selected six Leyland TS8s of 1938 and 1939 for rebodying by Plaxton with full-fronted bodies, numbering them 500-5.

They gave another seven years good service, before being withdrawn *en-bloc* in 1960 and sold on for further service. Number 502 (157), CTF 438 was photographed in its original red livery at Hindley depot, on the occasion of an Omnibus Society visit in 1956, and again outside Atherton depot in the later cream and red. With the exception of replacements for accident damaged vehicles, this was LUT's first rebodying exercise since the conversion of the Dennis charabancs during the mid-1920s. *(JAS, both)*

Six Guy Arab UFs with Weymann Hermes dual-purpose bodies and Gardner 6HLW engines arrived in 1954. They were real workhorses, being used extensively on the trunk Tyne Tees Mersey routes. The standard BET body shell sported a distinctive front end and seated 40. Number 518, STF 203, in red livery waits at Manchester's Lower Mosley Street bus station before continuing to Liverpool. The Bridgewater Concert Hall now stands on the site which for many years was a Mecca for enthusiasts, with a wide variety of operators using the facility and providing a fascinating selection of vehicle types and liveries. In the background is Central Railway Station, now the G-Mex Exhibition Centre. Number 521 in cream coach livery later in its life, is seen below on private hire. Two Leyland Tiger Cubs with standard BET Hermes bodies, Nos. 562/3, were also purchased, in 1955. *(GHFA, above)*

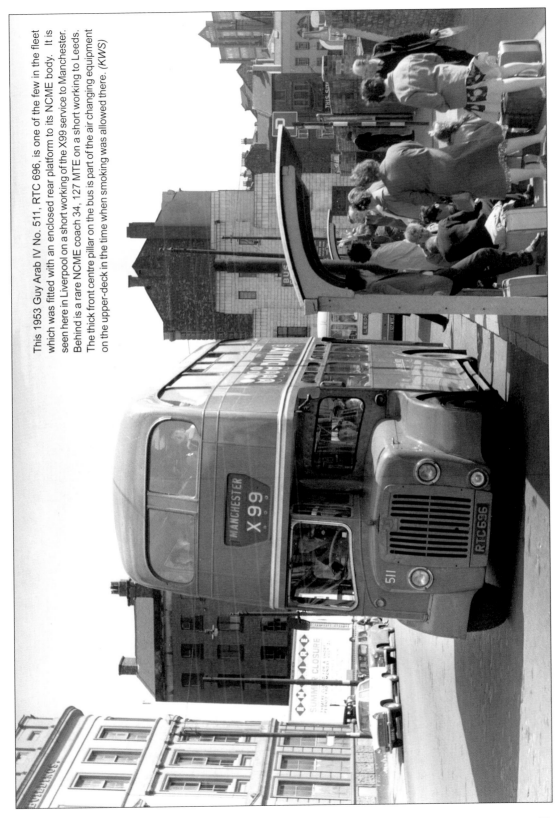

This 1953 Guy Arab IV No. 511, RTC 696, is one of the few in the fleet which was fitted with an enclosed rear platform to its NCME body. It is seen here in Liverpool on a short working of the X99 service to Manchester. Behind is a rare NCME coach 34, 127 MTE on a short working to Leeds. The thick front centre pillar on the bus is part of the air changing equipment on the upper-deck in the time when smoking was allowed there. (KWS)

Of particularly attractive appearance were these dual-purpose Atkinson Alphas with Roe 40-seat bodies (552-61, WTB 61-70), LUT's final batch of Atkinsons, received in 1955. The legal lettering proclaimed them to be owned by SLT and this view accentuates the high-backed moquette seating. Although intended for long-distance work, these vehicles could be seen equally on normal bus routes and on workmen's services in Trafford Park. Together with the 1955 Guy/NCME double-deckers seen opposite, they represented the last orders from Mr Edwardes. The garter-encircled Red Rose of Lancashire has not yet been applied to the front panel.

Brand new Atkinson/Roe semi-coach No. 552, WTB 61, complete with Red Rose emblem, outside Atherton depot on a bright Saturday afternoon, having just arrived on delivery with the trade plate still in the windscreen. Whilst the vehicle was cooling down after a fast run from Leeds heated words were taking place within the offices for what the camera doesn't show is the badly damaged rear nearside corner, following an unfortunate encounter with a stone wall *en route*. Doubtless the wall was to blame. Number 548, WTB 47, is shown below on route 42 from Bolton to Walkden. Part of the other 1955 order by Mr Edwardes, it was a standard Guy/NCME double-decker, also showing SLT as legal owner until 1st September 1958 when the legal lettering was changed to LUT. *(JAS both)*

A surprise event in 1955 was the rebodying of six of the wartime utilities, for although many operators regarded such exercises as normal, LUT did not. They lasted only 4-6 years longer than their unrebodied colleagues, casting considerable doubt on the value of the exercise. Numbers 300 and 306, both originally with Weymann bodies from the batch 298-307, FTE 31-40, were duly rebodied by NCME in 1955 and re-numbered 568 and 569, the former Roe lowbridge examples becoming 564-567. The pair lasted only to 1966 whereas the other Weymann utility bodied examples were withdrawn in 1962. Number 568, was caught on Atherton depot forecourt having just returned from the short run on route 29 between Shakerley Estate and Astley Village.

(JAS)

The last of the 1956 ten Arabs was No. 603, 320 ATC. Built to the newly legalised length of 30 ft., and seating 73 rather than the 64 of the other nine in the batch, it was displayed at the 1956 Commercial Motor Show at Earls Court, London, hence its chromed registration plate.

Five Duple coaches on Leyland Tiger Cub chassis arrived in 1957 (620-4, 951-5 BTF), the only vehicles to be purchased in that year. The 'Donnington' bodies were built at Duple's Midland factory. They gave good service, later being cascaded to bus work with some being painted in red bus livery including No. 623, 954 BTF. It is shown here at its regular destination, Blackpool's Colisuem coach station. After 13 years the batch was withdrawn, the last four passing to Douglas Corporation, Isle of Man where No. 623 was re-registered 230 UMN. *(JAS, both)*

No less than 30 Guy Arab IVs with NCME bodies were purchased in 1958 (604-19, 871-86 DTB and 630-43, 347-60 FTB). Number 613, 880 DTB waits at Warrington for its return journey on route 10 to Manchester – actually Salford, Greengate Arches, on the Manchester boundary, seen on page 74. (AEJ)

Mr Oakham asserted his influence in 1959 by changing the fleet numbering system. Leyland PD3/4 No. 657, 574 FTF became the highest number of the previous system which had lasted since 1936 with a few small deviations. This impressive bus (No. 652, 569 FTF) is one of a batch of 14 Leyland PD3/4s with Met-Cam bodies built to the 30ft. length (644-57, 561-74 FTF). They were purchased to replace the three-axled trolleybuses and thus needed a comparable seating capacity. The first of the batch was said to be the first PSV to have a fixed driver's windscreen after a change in the Construction & Use Regulations. The Oakham/Manchester influence is again apparent though Manchester never had any PD Titans of this length, almost certainly because the militant union members in the city fleet would not allow such large vehicles to be operated. Their day of reckoning eventually came with the arrival of the Atlanteans, but not without a prolonged dispute before the rear-engined vehicles were allowed on the road. The good old days?

A second batch of five Duple-bodied Leyland Tiger Cub coaches joined the fleet in 1958, similar to those of the previous year (625-9, 431-5 DTF). Again, four went to Douglas Corporation in 1970, including No. 629, 435 DTF seen in less-familiar Blackpool surroundings and which was re-registered 238 UMN when it reached the Island.

After the winding up of the SLT company, a new numbering system began. A further surprise was the arrival of five AEC Reliance coaches, Nos. 1-5. They were the first new AECs to be purchased since 1920 and were fitted with coach bodies, below, by the Blackpool coach builder HV Burlingham. They lasted until 1970. *(EO, JAS)*

When the SLT trolleybuses were withdrawn in August 1958 a fascinating era came to end. The vehicles in use included some, indeed most, of the original batch and dated back to 1930. There was no longer any need for the Company to continue generating electricity since it had, in any case, been supplying the CEGB and not its own customers as had been the case pre-1948. The vehicles were sold for scrap, including the four Bolton-owned examples, the overhead was soon removed and only the rusting traction poles, still used as street lighting supports, remained. Atherton depot was rebuilt to remove the traverser turntable and to make it more suitable for buses, including extending the workshop area.

The SLT mileage abandoned on 31st August 1958 was 18.75 and this covered two routes: Leigh-Atherton-Bolton, Atherton-Swinton-Farnworth. The St Helens service had been abandoned in 1956. At its peak SLT had 71 trolleybuses. At the end 33 were in service, the oldest being 28 years old. For some time before the closure, LUT motor buses had been standing in because of trolleybus mechanical faults. The 24 Daimler/Weymann 61-seat double-deckers were purchased to cover the Atherton to St. Helens route when the Corporation converted the St. Helens to Haydock section on 12th November 1956. For the final changeover LUT purchased a total of 30 73-seaters, 16 Guy/NCME (604-19,

871-86 DTB) and 14 Leyland Titan PD3/4 /Met-Cam. (644-57, 561-74 FTF).

LUT operated its first and last trolleybus for one day only on 1st September 1958. As the South Lancashire Transport Company went out of existence on the previous day, the last day of public service, the newest vehicle, No. 71, HTD 868, was licensed to LUT. It was repainted and specially lettered for the occasion of a commemorative run from Atherton to Leigh for local dignitaries. From Leigh a motor bus conveyed the party to the Brocket Arms Hotel in Wigan for a luncheon to celebrate the winding up of SLT. On its return journey to Atherton depot No. 71 carried members of the public free of charge. Sadly, this fine vehicle, only ten years old, passed with its fellows to a scrap dealer. The preservation movement had hardly started in 1958. Today there is a working trolleybus museum at Sandtoft near Doncaster.

Sir Joseph Nall, Chairman since 1955, died on 2nd May 1958 at the Annual General Meeting. He was succeeded by Mr HM Alderson Smith who himself died just prior to the demise of the SLT Company. Sir Robert Cary, Bart., MP was then appointed the new Chairman.

SLT's trolleybuses operated over three main 'tracks': from St Helens to Atherton; from Atherton to Farnworth via Swinton; and from Bolton to Leigh, also via Atherton. The St Helens route terminated just short of the Punchbowl, where vehicles from the other two routes could be seen.

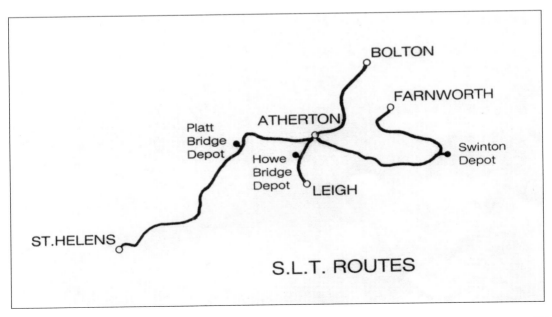

One of the first batch of ten trolleybuses dating from 1930, No. 9, TF 2080, a Guy BTX with MV motors and Roe lowbridge double-deck body seating 54, negotiates the complex wiring at the Atherton terminus of the St Helens route. As in many other locations a reversal across the road into a lay-by was involved, hence the wiring arrangements seen in the photograph. The conductor keeps a watchful eye on the approaching bus, though since it is an LUT one the driver will be aware of the potential movement. This vehicle was withdrawn in 1956 after the closure of the St Helens route though, at Ministry directive, the vehicles were stored in the yard alongside Atherton bus depot pending resolution of the Suez Crisis which threated to cut off oil supplies. Number 2, similarly largely unrebuilt, survived to the end in 1958 and was, briefly, the subject of an unsuccessful preservation attempt. Lack of storage space precluded progress. *(RB)*

Many of the original lowbridge trolleybuses were quite heavily rebuilt in the 1950s by Bond of Wythenshawe, Manchester. The degree of work involved varied from new fronts, as seen below on No. 1, in Platt Bridge depot yard in 1956, through new sides and rears, or any combination of these options. The first in the fleet, TF 2072 remained in service to the end, a very creditable performance indeed and one from which the shareholders benefited. *(JAS)*

Photographer Roy Brook must have been wondering how long it would be before the heavens opened when he took this shot of a St Helens vehicle at the Atherton terminus, soon after his other view seen opposite. Note that the St Helens vehicles displayed route numbers, whereas SLT's did not. Number 313 was a Sunbeam W model with Roe lowbridge bodywork, dating from 1945.

SLT Trolleybuses Nos. 55 and 56, DTC 262-3, 1938 Leyland TTB4s with Metro-Vickers motors and Roe bodies seating 64 standing at Spinning Jenny Street terminus in Leigh before returning to Bolton. The batch, Nos. 54-9, lasted until the end of the system, thus completing 20 years service. Note that whilst No. 56 retains the small shaded numerals its compatriot sports the later plain gold numerals with black outline. *(RB, both)*

The local photographer from *The Journal* group turned out to photograph the last trolleybus to leave Farnworth. There was little ceremony other than this. Map maker and transport historian John Gillham peers through the sliding window, whilst a youthful John Senior stands third from the left, ready to rejoin colleague Alan Drabble for the final run.

After the other passengers had disembarked there was time for another photograph to record the event as trolleybus No. 28, TF 5807, waited for its last trip from Swinton depot after the final service journey from Farnworth on 31st August 1958. That move took place in the early hours of September 1st and the driver came out of the depot with trade plates since the vehicle was no longer licensed following the demise of the SLT company at midnight. Note the paper sticker bearing the sad epithet 'To Atherton with the compliments of Swinton'. *(JAS)*

The last trolleybus in the fleet and the last to run, No. 71, HTD 868, a 1948 Karrier MS2 with Weymann 64-seat body at Atherton depot on 1st September 1958. The legal lettering records that this is Lancashire United's first and last trolleybus, licensed for the one day to carry the local councillors and other invited guests on one final trip.

At the Manchester LRTL meeting in September, the late Gwynne Thomas provided John Senior with the opportunity to take what is believed to be the only photograph of the four Bolton Corporation-owned Leyland TTB4/Roe trolleybuses, SLT fleet Nos. 48-51, ATE 792-5 after withdrawal in August 1958 and parked for the first time at Bolton's Bridgeman Street depot yard. Note the various stages of rebuild. They were sold for scrap to Birds of Stratford-upon-Avon. *(JAS)*

The Dennis Loline was produced under licence from Bristol, incorporating the patented design which allowed the body to sit much lower on the chassis, and thereby reduced the overall height of the vehicle. The sunken lower deck gangway can be seen in the interior view, above, and it will be immediately apparent that there is no intruding upper-deck gangway. The unpopular layout, which dated back to the Leyland Titans which first entered

the fleet in 1929, had finally met its match. LUT took two from Dennis Bros in Guildford, bodied by NCME, in 1959, numbered 6 and 7 as seen opposite, and a further four the following year. The rear-engined Fleetline then became a better option with its front entrance under the supervision of the driver and it too was able to accommodate a low height body which could pass below low railway bridges without having the side-gangway in the upper saloon.

The Dennis Loline, opposite and above, had provided one answer to the unpopular lowbridge layout, of which there were still many examples in the fleet. By 1960 a wholesale clearout was to take place, with most of the utility buses and the remaining pre-war double-deckers being sold for scrap. Included amongst the survivors were the last of the 1937 Titan TD5s, some of which had given 23 years service. Number 66, still with original body, is seen here looking typically smart when photographed two or three years earlier. This was a typical Saturday afternoon scene in Atherton depot at that time. (JAS)

Another survivor until the 1960 cull was this TD4 which had originally carried a Leyland metal-framed V-front body. It had been involved in a serious accident. The chassis was rebodied by Northern Counties and No. 53 is seen here on a Saturday afternoon rugby special at Swinton in the mid-1950s. Standing in line can be seen a Dennis Lance, then a Roe-bodied Guy UF coach; beyond them were several more LUT single-deckers with more buses in all the streets around – bus photography was easy on winter Saturdays provided that it wasn't foggy or raining with the slow film of the day. (JAS)

A batch of ten Daimler CSG6/30 double-deckers was purchased in 1959 with 30 ft NCME 73-seat bodies. This view of No. 16 illustrates a characteristic location for a LUT double-decker. It is seen at the Blackpool Coliseum coach station, having arrived from Manchester on the famous X60 service. The CSG code indicates a synchromesh gearbox which Daimler offered as an alternative to its more usual preselective transmission. *(EO coll)*

The customary Guy Arab IV/NCME double-deckers also came in 1959 with fleet Nos. 18-27 and No. 19 is seen on route 38 from Salford Greengate to Westhoughton, a short working on the route to Wigan. Gardner 6LW engines were fitted except for the last one of the batch, No. 27, which was the only Arab IV with the later 6LX engine. Manchester-style livery has now become firmly established. Number 19 was withdrawn in 1977. *(AEJ)*

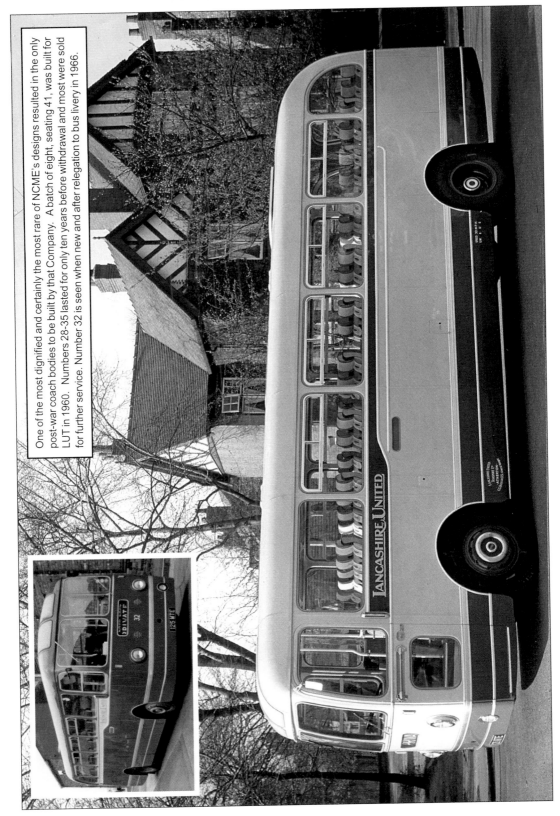

One of the most dignified and certainly the most rare of NCME's designs resulted in the only post-war coach bodies to be built by that Company. A batch of eight, seating 41, was built for LUT in 1960. Numbers 28-35 lasted for only ten years before withdrawal and most were sold for further service. Number 32 is seen when new and after relegation to bus livery in 1966.

A batch of ten 73-seat Met-Cam bodies was purchased in 1961 on 30 ft Guy Arab IV chassis, Nos. 40-9, and number 41 is seen on a short working on route 39 from Leigh to Salford Greengate. Behind is Daimler Fleetline No. 99 on the entire journey from Liverpool via St. Helens, Newton le Willows and Atherton to 'Manchester,' or more correctly, Salford Greengate. *(AEJ)*

Eight Guy Arab IVs with NCME bodies of 1960 comprised more usual fare. The batch was numbered 50-7 and No. 52 was photographed on route 26 from Leigh to Salford Greengate. The more attractive lines of the NCME body are immediately apparent, and bodies from the MCW organisation were very much in a minority with LUT – maybe just to keep NCME on their toes pricewise. *(AEJ)*

Being an enthusiastic Guy operator, LUT ordered three of the new Wulfrunian chassis in 1961. Guy was attempting to produce a front entrance bus in the style of the Leyland Atlantean and Daimler Fleetline but with the engine at the front which was regarded as proven engineering practice, especially as problems had been encountered with the early rear-engined examples. Other problems soon appeared on the Wulfrunian such as poor weight distribution due to the heavy Gardner engine positioned ahead of the front wheels, early disc brakes and air suspension, and insufficient platform space. Too many advanced and unusual features soon led to a poor reputation for the Wulfrunian and only ten were sold to operators other than the West Riding Automobile Company (another large independent) which had collaborated in its design. Only one Wulfrunian was delivered to LUT, No. 58, 802 RTC, in 1961 and this was withdrawn the following year and sold to the West Riding company. The two cancelled Wulfrunians were replaced with two tried and tested Guy Arab IVs, Nos. 59-60, 565-6 VTJ. It was reported that they were built with Gardner's new 6LX engines but were changed to 6LWs before entering service. Eventually both Guy Motors and West Riding were to succumb. The rear view is taken outside the original NCME works in Wigan Lane, with the bay windows of the house clearly visible.

LUT's choice when it bought its first rear-engined double-deckers in 1962 was the Daimler Fleetline, no doubt due to the availability of the Gardner engine. Another factor would have been the overall height, which was lower than the contemporary Leyland Atlantean, having regard to the many low railway bridges in the operating area. Here, No. 99 is on route 39 between Liverpool and Manchester via St. Helens, Leigh, Atherton and Worsley with a journey time of 2 hrs. 15 mins. This bus survived with LUT for 19 years despite an accident in 1977 and an engine fire in 1979. In other hands it completed a total service life of 28 years. *(AEJ)*

More Guy Arab IVs came in 1962 including No. 116, pictured here on former trolleybus route 1, St Helens to Atherton via Haydock, Ashton in Makerfield and Hindley. Both buses on this page have NCME bodies. *(GL)*

LUT's exhibit at the 1962 Commercial Motor Show in London's Earls Court was Daimler Fleetline No. 137, 8100 TD on the Northern Counties stand. Gardner 6LX engines of 10.45 litres capacity were fitted to LUT's Fleetlines which provided good performance with economy. Number 137 was withdrawn after 13 years.

A reversion to Leyland for the 36ft chassis order came in 1964 with the bus and dual-purpose bodies again by Plaxton. Numbers 151-5 (d.p.) and 156-8 (bus) were on Leopard PSU3/3R chassis whilst this example, No. 151, DTF 581B, suffered fire damage in 1975 and was withdrawn. (GLC)

More Guys entered the fleet each year from 1963 to 1967, now the Arab V, available in 27ft and 30ft lengths. These too employed the Gardner 6LX engine. Having a lower frame than the Arab IV, this chassis was better suited to forward-entrance applications, though the traditional rear platform was available. Both versions accommodated 73 seated passengers, and No. 132 is a 'back loading' example. It is waiting at Warrington for the return journey to Manchester via Cadishead, Irlam and Eccles, a journey which would take it 1hr 15min. *(AEJ, both)*

Twelve Guy Arab Vs with B and C suffix registrations were taken into stock in 1964-5, numbered 159-70, and number 170 was the Commercial Motor Show exhibit in 1964. Number 162 leaves Bolton, below, on the longer route to Salford, Greengate via the A6 road and Little Hulton, Walkden, Roe Green and Worsley. Henceforth all NCME bodies on Guy Arab Vs would be forward-entrance. The lack of glazing behind the driver's cab in the first bay confirms the position of the staircase, and hence the entrance.

LUT took standard Plaxton coach bodies on Leyland L2
Leopard chassis with O.600 engines in 1965. Here,
No. 202 competes in that year's Blackpool Coach Rally.

Front entrance buses provided more space for rear advertisements as this Arab V demonstrates . . . *(AEJ, above)*

Number 241, YTD 249D, was a one-off vehicle built by Northern Counties on a Leyland Tiger Cub chassis for the NCME stand at the 1966 Commercial Motor Show at Earls Court, London.

The two-door 40-seat body on No. 241 provided space for another 16 standing passengers. It remained the only vehicle of its type in the fleet. This would have been an obvious candidate for preservation but it met an untimely end being burnt out by vandals in 1979.

Guy Arab V/NCME No. 274, ETJ 910F, of LUT's 1967 and last batch of Guys, laying over at Warrington awaiting its return to Manchester (Salford, Greengate) on the long-established service 10. Behind is a Daimler Fleetline of GMT with NCME body to the PTE's standard design and livery, No. 7408, YNA 363M of 1974. *(AEJ)*

Government policy, encouraging operators by grants towards the purchase of new buses, brought about a radical change in bus design in its promotion of one-man-operation (o-m-o). Specifications were laid down for grant eligibility which resulted in the demise of front-engined double-deck production. In a final bid LUT purchased a batch of 26 of its favoured Guy Arab Vs with 73-seat NCME forward-entrance bodies, Nos. 265-90, ETJ 901-26F in 1967. There were no more double-deckers until the rear-engined Daimler Fleetlines in 1971, and all further double-deckers were of this make (or its Leyland successor) until the final entrants in 1980. A mixed bag of single-deckers joined the fleet between these dates including Seddon RUs, Bristol REs, Leyland Leopards, all with Plaxton bodies, and Leyland Nationals. Seddon was another Lancashire manufacturer, based at Royton near Oldham, better known for its heavy goods vehicles. Two large batches were purchased, Nos. 338-357, WTD 671-90H, in 1970 and Nos. 364-393, DTJ 712-741J, in 1971 but few lasted more than eleven years. LUT certainly supported its home county with its purchases of most of its chassis, bodies and engines, thus maintaining local employment.

A new Transport Act in 1968 brought enormous changes to the British bus industry. The Act required the establishment of Passenger Transport Authorities and Executives in the main conurbations one of which was the South East Lancashire and North East Cheshire area to become known as SELNEC. Briefly, the Authority was to determine policy and the Executive was to operate services in accordance with that policy.

The SELNEC PTE took over the undertakings of the eleven municipal operators in its area on 1st November 1969. LUT was interwoven into this network since it operated within and without the area and operated joint services with three of the absorbed municipalities, Salford, Bolton and Leigh. In 1970 a working agreement was announced between LUT and SELNEC by which the Company's stage services were co-ordinated with those of the PTE. Another agreement in 1971 provided inter alia for the Company to pay certain revenues to the Executive, the Executive to determine fares and frequencies of co-ordinated services, and payment of operating costs to the Company, all to commence with effect from 1st January 1971. Finally, the Executive had the option to purchase the share capital of the Company on 31st December 1975. From 1971 PTE officers were appointed to the Board and the Company became the PTE's agent to provide certain services within the PTE's area.

As each authority had its own route numbering system the attempt to introduce an area wide scheme was at first chaotic and it took four years to develop a suitable one. This resulted in many LUT services being re-numbered though some retained their LUT numbers including the Salford to Bolton services 8 and 12, Salford to Wigan 32 and 38 and Salford to Liverpool 39. Most LUT services were re-numbered in the 500 and 600 series.

The 1968/9 Bristol REs numbered 294-313 carried bodywork by Alexander of Falkirk. The AEC Swifts, 291-3, bodied by the same manufacturer, were sold to St Helens after only five years, but the Bristols gave twelve years service. These were the only Alexander bodies purchased.

LUT took a batch of 20 Seddon RUs with Plaxton 40-seat dual-door bus bodies in 1970. Number 339, WTD 672H, above, was caught by the camera in Trafford Park. *(MRK)*

A dual-door double-decker with ordinary bus seats was, perhaps, not the most agreeable means of making a two and a quarter hour journey from Manchester to Blackpool but every type of vehicle, coach or bus, was pressed into service on the X60/X70 routes on summer weekends. This 76-seat NCME-bodied Daimler Fleetline No. 361, ATJ 275J, is parked up at the usual spot in the Coliseum coach station in June, 1972. *(EO)*

LUT took 33ft-long Daimler Fleetlines, and specified the enclosed rear, eliminating the engine pod. They were also two-door, as can be seen, and thus differed in several respects from Manchester's Fleetlines. Number 412 had very recently been delivered from Northern Counties when it was posed for the photographer. (JAS)

After a switch from cream to grey for the secondary colour, the 1974 batch of the highly-regarded Bristol RE chassis with Gardner engines and Plaxton bodies was turned out in a reversed version of this livery. Number 414, TTB 445M, seen above, waits outside the main garage at Howe Bridge. *(JAS)*

Another NCME one-off was Leyland Leopard No. 424, GBN 331N, below, built for the 1974 Commercial Motor Show but no more were made to this design. It is pictured here in the later GMT livery of orange with white roof and brown skirt. For the Show the livery was red and grey with an enlarged 'Lancashire United' fleetname in the deep grey band below the windows. It was not one of NCME's better designs. *(AEJ)*

A splendid view of one of the last batch of vehicles delivered to the independent Company in 1975. The Leyland PSU3C/4R Leopard with 44-seat dual-door body was one of the last composite bodies built by Plaxton. A batch of 35 had been ordered, Nos. 430-64 and only five, Nos. 430-34, were delivered before the takeover. Only the first two were of this configuration; the rest were single-door but still with 44 seats.

Closer liaison with Selnec PTE resulted from an agreement of 1972 which brought in the private company Lanaten Ltd. associated with LUT's main body builder NCME and with Henry Gethin Lewis as a Director of both. During that year the PTE sought further discussions with the Board of LUT which resulted in an offer by Lanaten Ltd. for the purchase of the whole of the share capital of the Company. After taking advice from its merchant bankers, Kleinwort Benson, the Board agreed to recommend the offer to shareholders. In order to bring this about the PTE guaranteed a loan which Lanaten had negotiated with Schroders. At that time LUT was a 'quoted' company on the London Stock Exchange and there were no large individual shareholdings.

It was announced in June 1972 that Lanaten's bid of £2.5 million for LUT had been successful and had the full support of the PTA. LUT's operations were to be pooled with the PTE and all receipts were to be paid to the PTE. The PTE was to pay defined expenses to the Company including provision for depreciation. In the event of the exercise of the PTE's option to purchase LUT the price payable by the PTE for the whole of the issued share capital would be £2,650,000 or such sum as the auditors of Lanaten Ltd. certified as being the cost of the acquisition. GM Robert Bailey stated later that it was, in fact, slightly less than this amount and, therefore, closer to Lanaten's original bid.

In an agreement of June 1973 express services from Manchester to Blackpool and Blackburn and from Liverpool to Newcastle passed to Ribble, and the Warrington local services operated jointly with Warrington Corporation passed to Crosville.

Certain Ribble services passed to LUT as did some SELNEC services from Bolton. LUT closed its Liverpool office and discontinued the garaging of coaches at the former LCPT Edge Lane depot which now belonged to Merseyside PTE.

Local government reorganisation, effective from 1st April 1974, brought a change of name to the PTA and PTE, now prefixed with 'Greater Manchester,' and brought Wigan into the area with its municipal bus undertaking. Greater Manchester County was created consisting of the twelve authorities and the word 'countywide' was the buzz-word of the local politicians. However, this enlarged authority was short-lived, being abolished in 1986 after a change of national government when the former constituents became unitary authorities.

By 1974 only a few LUT operations remained outside the enlarged PTE area. The services in Warrington were by now operated wholly by Warrington Corporation and no services were operated completely outside the area. The stage was set, therefore, for GMPTE to exercise its option to purchase LUT which it did with effect from 1st January 1976. LUT became a wholly-owned subsidiary of GMPTE to operate for the time-being as a separate entity. Fleet strength at this date was 371 vehicles.

The last vehicles purchased by the independent company were five Leyland Leopards with Plaxton bus bodies, two with dual doors and three with single door, Nos. 430-4, JDK 921-5P. In fact 35 of these distinctive vehicles had been ordered, being among the last Plaxton bodies of composite construction to be built, the balance of 30 being delivered after the takeover. Thus this much-loved and undoubtedly distinctive bus company continued to demonstrate its individuality and proclaim its true county for more years to come, since many of these buses survived in service until 1995.

After the delivery of the previously-ordered Leyland/Plaxton buses in 1976, normal purchases for LUT by Greater Manchester Transport settled down to Daimler (Leyland from 1977) Fleetline double-deckers and Leyland National single-deckers. Since the latter were available only in poppy red or green livery for NBC fleets, London Transport red and all-over white, LUT took them in all-over LT red which was slightly darker than the normal Company red but looked well with the long-standing 'Lancashire United' fleetname in gold. All double-deckers of course carried NCME bodies. In fact, most double-deckers since 1949 and all since 1961 were bodied by NCME. Later, after the takeover, NCME bodies to the standard PTE design began to appear in LUT red and grey.

Small batches of coaches were taken into stock, all Leyland Leopards with Plaxton bodies, Nos. 480-4 in 1977, 537-41 in 1978 and 566-9 in 1979. A surprise in 1980 was the arrival of the first foreign chassis since the Fiats of 1920 when three Volvo B58s with Plaxton bodies were purchased. PTE coach livery consisted of basic white with coloured stripes going up over the roof, the colour of the stripes varying according to the coaching unit. Thus the PTE's Charterplan unit used orange and brown and the LUT coaches used red and yellow. Different coloured stripes were used for the other two acquired coaching units, Godfrey Abbott of Sale and Warburtons of Bury.

LUT had used the traditional TIM ticket machines for many years and these were phased out in favour of the PTE standard Almex machines. The independent LUT had tried the Videmat system on the former trolleybus route 582, Leigh-Atherton-Bolton, and this too was replaced with Almex machines.

The second delivery of Fleetlines in 1978, Nos. 515-29, appeared in a variation of the GMT livery of orange and white with plain Lancashire United Transport fleetnames. This variation featured a larger area of orange, and then single-deckers began to appear in orange with a white roof. Sadly, the stylish fleetname, unchanged since the mid-1920s, and the red rose of Lancashire enclosed within a garter, were dropped in favour of the GMT logo known as the M-blem. The LUT fleet numbering scheme continued for the present.

There was no doubt that the end was approaching when the M-blem appeared on the former LUT vehicles.

Lancashire United's Nationals looked smart in the dark red, but engineer Graham Dewhurst had resisted the marque until his hand was forced; he would have preferred to continue purchasing the more reliable Bristol RE chassis but Leyland would not supply these to home market customers, thus making them take Nationals. The earlier batch had the LUT garter on the front. (AEJ)

A more disturbing sign of changing times is this contrast in Company names at the Atherton Head Office. The new order is represented by the somewhat flimsy painted board whilst above the doorway, defiant to the last, the original name can still be seen in the stonework. This important piece of history was preserved for posterity, but, sadly, is all that remains of the Atherton complex.

A view in Swinton depot showing two of the Plaxton-bodied Leopards which had been purchased to avoid buying Nationals, despite their high floors making them rather unsuitable for bus work. The change of livery can0 clearly be seen. One remained in service until 1995, being the last of the former LUT vehicles so to do. Two of the batch survive in preservation. *(JAS, both)*

Small numbers of coaches continued to be put into the fleet by the PTE after takeover until 1981, whilst LUT continued to be operated as a separate unit. The 1977 batch consisted of five Leyland Leopards with Plaxton bodies of which No. 484, OTD 828R, was the last. It was fitted with tables and curtains in 1981 for use as the team coach for Swinton Rugby League Football Club. It remained for only two more years before being sold for further service.

A more suitable vehicle for the Blackpool run was this Leyland Leopard/Plaxton which was the last of the batch of five for 1978. Number 541, TWH 689T, was sold in 1984 but went on to complete a service life of over 20 years in other hands. These two pictures illustrate the PTE coach livery with stripes running up over the roof on a white base. The PTE's various coaching units used stripes of different colours as mentioned. LUT's colours were red and yellow. The floodlights of Blackpool Football Club's Bloomfield Road ground can be seen in the background of Rigby Road coach park. *(EO, both)*

Under the new ownership staff conditions and wages were integrated and staff were taken into the GMT superannuation scheme. Conductor operation lingered until January 1982 in order that the Guy Arabs might complete the then GMT service life of 13 years, much less than the LUT policy which saw many buses serve for 20 years. In fact some Fleetlines did survive for 19 and 20 years.

Perhaps the greatest surprise was the purchase in 1980 of 20 ex-London Transport Daimler Fleetlines of the DMS class from the Essex dealer Ensign at a cost of £7,000 each. The announcement at the GMC Transport Committee angered Labour councillors who claimed the purchase could harm employment in the Wigan area. It took another 20 years, however, in completely different times, before the Northern Counties factory was closed down by Alexander Dennis. These 1972-3 buses with MCW and Park Royal bodies had their centre doors removed by Ensign before delivery bringing the seating capacity to 71. They were the first second-hand buses since the ex-Liverpool AECs bought in 1922 except for vehicles taken over with acquired operators. The DMSs gave a good account of themselves but all were withdrawn by 1985, perhaps in line with the GMT 13-year policy.

In 1980 LUT's final vehicles consisted of a batch of 25 Leyland FE30AGR Fleetlines with NCME 75-seat bodies to PTE specification, Nos. 589-613, DWH 682-706W, which brought the fleet numbering system to a close. The last vehicle of all, No. 613, DWH 706W, passed to the SELNEC Preservation Society in 1998.

Officially, the end of LUT came on 31st March 1981 when the Company was wound up, the fleet merged with that of GMT and the fleetname disappeared. The addition of the 360 LUT vehicles brought the GMT fleet strength up to more than 2,600 and the 1,400 LUT employees became part of the GMT staff. The LUT works, depot, office complex *et al* at Howe Bridge was closed in 1998 and later razed to the ground.

So ended this distinctive and individualistic independent company. While its stage operating area was comparatively small, being bounded by Liverpool, Wigan, Bolton, Warrington and Manchester, the fleetname could be seen countrywide on its extensive coaching activities on express routes and private hire. During its history LUT vehicles reached such diverse places as Glasgow, Bournemouth, London, Skegness and the North Wales coast holiday resorts. Fortunately, some former LUT vehicles have been preserved and can be seen around the country on the rally scene in the once familiar red and cream livery with the long-standing fleetname style and the proud red Lancashire rose.

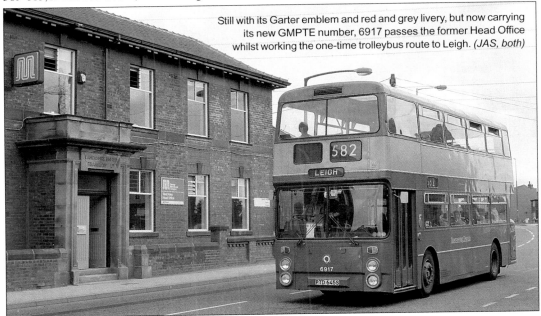

Still with its Garter emblem and red and grey livery, but now carrying its new GMPTE number, 6917 passes the former Head Office whilst working the one-time trolleybus route to Leigh. *(JAS, both)*

Now looking somewhat unkempt and rather unloved former LUT Fleetline number 410 awaits its next duty in Swinton depot. In the background one of the GM 8xxx series shows the brown skirted version of the GMT livery. The 33ft-long example is a sorry reflection of its former proud state when delivered in the attractive LUT red and grey livery as shown on page 118. *(JAS)*

The former London Transport Fleetlines fitted into LUT's vehicle pattern quite well, and were undoubtedly a good investment. They performed well and demonstrated, again, that with suitable maintenance they were robust and reliable. The registration MLH 458L shows the origin of number 333, seen working the long-established Manchester to Bolton service 12. Above the fleet number the letters SN indicate its depot allocation – Swinton. Needless to say, perhaps, this was not an ex-LUT practice. *(EO)*

Leyland National No. 560 is seen in Partington Lane, outside the Swinton depot where it was then based, but by that time carrying GMPTE orange and white livery. It is working the former trolleybus route from Farnworth to Atherton, numbered 583 after conversion to motor bus operation. *(JAS)*

Three liveries in one picture on the PTE's standard body design. Former LUT 600 is in the orange and white version carried by its vehicles whilst behind it one of the GMT fleet, also with NCME bodywork, shows the standard application of the colour scheme. In the distance another LUT vehicle is still in the original red and grey livery. (JAS)

Personalities

Lancashire United Transport was notable for the commitment of its Directors and Officers and the loyalty of its staff. Many employees served for remarkably long periods and numerous families had two or even three generations working for the Company. Reference has already been made to the Thirty Club. The membership in 1963 was 254 who had served for over thirty years with 177 still on the active list, and four members had completed 50 years of service.

Of the Directors and Officers, while Sir Arthur Stanley had been the moving and guiding force behind the Company for 42 years, and John Soame Austen, while remaining a 'back room boy', had been its financial brains for 35 years, the Company's most outstanding character was undoubtedly its General Manager, then Managing Director and Chairman, Edward Henry Edwardes, known as 'Ned' He not only held office for 44 years before retiring at the age of 80 in 1955 but became one of the best known figures in the British passenger transport industry.

EDWARD HENRY EDWARDES

Born on 18th February 1875, Ned Edwardes was the youngest son of the Reverend the Hon. Thomas Edwardes of Horncastle, Lincolnshire. He was educated at Marlborough College, Wiltshire, and in 1907 married Eleanor Matilda, the daughter of the Reverend William Nuttall of Atherton. They had five children, three boys and two girls. One daughter, Barbara, married AH Gernaey in 1939 who became Chief Engineer of LUT in 1949. The other daughter, Nora, married Hugh Gardner, a Director of the family company L Gardner & Sons Ltd. There was thus a family connection between LUT and its main diesel engine supplier. Edwardes's early electrical training was with Robey of Lincoln. His first appointment was with another LUT, London United Tramways, where Theodore Thomas was his assistant. Later, Sir Theodore became head of the London company and then General Manager of the London Passenger Transport Board, and Ned remained in touch with him over the years. In 1946, after his retirement from London Transport, Thomas became a Director of Lancashire United until his death in 1951. Edwardes joined SLT from London United Tramways in 1901 as resident Engineer and then Power Station Engineer. He was appointed General Manager of both SLT and LUT at the beginning of 1911 following the death of JR Salter the previous month. On his appointment as Managing Director in 1932 the post of General Manager was discontinued. He became Chairman in 1947. Remaining in office until he was 80 years of age his interest in the industry never flagged and his knowledge of passenger transport was always up to date. He was a great fighter for the industry and no one with any sense ever tried to fool him. His leadership brought success and prosperity to his Company and he was beloved by his staff.

Ned Edwardes enjoyed the industry's social events and he was a keen ballroom dancer. Very much the Edwardian gentleman he indulged in the sports of golf, shooting and fishing when it was not unknown for him to fall in the water. He played golf weekly and took golfing weekends with friends several times a year. Other interests were gardening at his Worsley home, music and his Presidency of the Leigh Arts Council. Bridge and dominoes were his evening relaxations and he loved a good argument. It was said that if he was rude to you he liked you; it was never safe to believe that he was as hard of hearing as he professed to be; and it was less safe to think that he was necessarily asleep!

Transport historian Charles F Klapper said of him, "Any impression that he was not fully awake was an illusion eagerly fostered by Ned." His sense of humour made him an amusing after-dinner speaker. He retained the firm Christian faith into which he was born and he was strongly patriotic. All in all a great English character but with a sound business and technical head. He retired in April 1955 and died on 5th November of the same year aged 80.

Sir ARTHUR STANLEY

Born on 18th November 1869, he was the third son of the 16th Earl of Derby. Educated at Wellington College, Berkshire, he was employed in the Diplomatic Service and the Foreign Office. He became Private Secretary to Arthur James Balfour, the First Lord of the Treasury, in 1892,

Ned Edwardes in relaxed mood. *(EO coll)*

then a Secretary in the Diplomatic Service in Cairo. He became Conservative Member of Parliament for Ormskirk in 1898 and held the seat until he retired in 1918. Chairman of SLT from 1902, he was Chairman of LUT from its registration in December 1905 until his death in 1947. Among his other chairmanships were the British Red Cross Society, 1914-43; the Royal Automobile Club, 1905-7 and 1912-36; and the Royal College of Nursing. He was also a Justice of the Peace and Deputy Lieutenant for Lancashire. He lived in Eastbourne, Sussex and died on 4th November 1947.

JOHN SOAME AUSTEN

Born in 1862, educated at Felsted and Cambridge, Austen trained as a solicitor and first appears in this story as a stockbroker and trust-fund manager working from an office in Dashwood House, close to London's stock exchange, with which he was clearly closely associated. He was a Director, and in many cases also Chairman, of a multiplicity of companies, including, from 1906, Lancashire United Tramways Ltd. Other Directorships listed in 1913 included South Lancashire Tramway Company, New St Helens & District Tramways Co Ltd, the Venezuela Telephone & Electrical Appliances Co Ltd, and the International Russian Corporation Ltd. He was 'number two' to Emil Garcke, the BET boss, and Austen's 'number two' was HC Drayton. When Garcke retired as BET's Chairman in 1920 Austen took his place.

Roger Fulford, in his history of the BET records that 'Austen never had a desk in his life, doing all his work at a board-room table without any elaborate equipment. He was known to conclude the terms of a large financial deal on the back of an old envelope from the waste paper basket.' By 1931 the list of his business interests was prodigious, with copper, transport and finance being at the heart of them all. The Director's listing for that year gives an indication of the spread; his British interests included Chairmanship of the

British Electric Traction Company (BET), Western Welsh Omnibus Co Ltd, Electrical & Investment Co Ltd, Government & General Investment Co Ltd, Colonial Securities Co Ltd, and the International Finance Society Ltd, together with a string of Directorships in South America and his Russian connection, some of which he also chaired.

He attended his last LUT board meeting in June 1940 and died 18 months later on 12th January 1942. The BET history records him as a man who kept out of the limelight, but he was, without doubt, the man who financed Sir Arthur Stanley's needs for the growth and stability of the Lancashire United company. One might wonder just how he kept so many business interests under control simultaneously, but clearly he did so, and extremely successfully.

Sir JOSEPH NALL

Sir ROBERT ARCHIBALD CARY.

Sir Robert Cary was born on 25th May 1898, the son of a publican from working class West Hampstead. He was educated at Ardingly and the Royal Military College, Sandhurst. He served in both World Wars on the General Staff with the Royal Dragoon Guards, from 1916-23 and from 1939-45. After the Armistice in 1918 he served in Iraq and Persia until 1923, rejoining in September 1939. He married in 1924 the Hon. Rosamond Mary Curzon, daughter of Col the Hon. Alfred Curzon and sister of Viscount Scarsdale. They had one son, Roger Hugh, born in 1926. He was Conservative MP for Eccles from 1935-45 and for Withington, Manchester from 1951-74. He was knighted in 1945. He held several Government posts including a full Whip and PPS to the Minister of Health, the Lord Privy Seal and Leader of the House. He was described as a kind and modest man with no love of the limelight but he fought hard for the things he believed in. Sir Robert was appointed Chairman of LUT in 1958 in succession to Mr HM Alderson Smith who had died. At this time the other Directors were FA Willink, GFF Davies and JM Birch. Sir Robert lived in Wrotham, Kent and died on 1st October 1979 aged 81.

Sir JOSEPH NALL

Born on 24th August 1887 in Worsley, the son of Joseph Nall, he was educated privately and became a Director of several transport undertakings including LUT in 1942. He was Chairman of the Llandudno and Colwyn Bay Electric Railway Ltd., Midland General Omnibus Co. Ltd., Mansfield District Traction Co., and Notts and Derby Traction Co. He became Chairman of LUT in 1955 succeeding EH Edwardes. In 1916 he married Edith Elizabeth Francklin of Gonalston, Nottinghamshire and they had two sons and three daughters. He became Unionist MP for Hulme, Manchester from 1918-29 and 1931-45. He served in the First World War in Egypt, Gallipoli and France, was wounded, mentioned in despatches and awarded the DSO in 1918. He also served in the Second World War and retired from the Territorial Army as a Colonel in 1948. He was appointed Deputy Lieutenant of Lancashire and High Sheriff of Nottinghamshire in 1952 and was a Past President of the Institute of Transport and a Past Chairman of the Public Transport Association. He was also a Justice of the Peace for Nottinghamshire. He lived at Hoveringham Hall, Notts. and died on 2nd May 1958 aged 70.

CYRIL CHARLES OAKHAM

Cyril Oakham had an unusually comprehensive career covering both the manufacturing and operating sides of the industry and experience with trams, trolleybuses and motor buses. Born on

30th May 1905 he commenced work with London County Council before the formation in 1933 of the London Passenger Transport Board. Here he had experience with the trams and later the trolleybuses. He joined AEC as Traction Engineer in 1945, becoming Chief Engineer of its trolleybus manufacturing associate British United Traction Ltd. before moving to the municipal sector with Newcastle upon Tyne Corporation as Rolling Stock Engineer in 1949. Two years later he moved to Manchester Corporation as Chief Engineer. His move to the private sector came in 1955 as General Manager of LUT in succession to EH Edwardes, becoming a Director in 1961. It was a considerable surprise to the industry when he announced his retirement in 1964. Sir Robert Cary, the Chairman, stated that the retirement arose as a result of a difference of opinion which led to 'exchanges' between Mr Oakham and members of the Board. At the annual general meeting in 1964 it was decided to pay Mr Oakham £10,000 for loss of office. Only one shareholder dissented. Worsley Urban District Council opposed an application for higher fares because of the 'golden handshake' to Mr Oakham and the Company's

profit made in 1963. It is understood that Mr Oakham set up in business as a garage proprietor. He was succeeded by Robert Bailey

ROBERT BAILEY

Bob Bailey, born at Finedon, Northamptonshire on 25th September 1913, commenced his transport career as a clerk with the United Counties Omnibus Company Ltd. in 1929 at a wage of 12s. 6d. per week. Up to 1940 he played rugby for Wellingborough. He progressed to Traffic Superintendent, Express Services, and then spent the war years in the Royal Army Service Corps attaining the rank of Major with control of 150 vehicles. He served in the Middle East, Italy and Austria. After the war he moved to Northern General Transport Co. Ltd. at Gateshead as Assistant Traffic Manager, then to Potteries Motor Traction Co. Ltd. at Stoke on Trent as Traffic Manager in 1955. It was from this post that he was appointed in 1964 as General Manager of LUT becoming a Director two years later.

When LUT was taken over by GMPTE in 1976, Bob Bailey joined the Executive Committee as Commercial Services Executive and became Chairman of several wholly-owned subsidiary companies. He served on the Council of the Confederation of British Road Passenger Transport becoming Vice-President in 1974. He was also a past Chairman of the Passenger Road Transport Association, a member of the National Council for the Omnibus Industry and of the Conference of Omnibus Companies. In 1978 he was awarded the MBE, and retired at the age of 64 after 49 years in the industry to enjoy his hobbies of golf and gardening. Married with three daughters, he died in 1990.

Mr Oakham, camera in hand, poses with local dignitaries and former Secretary Jacob Holt, left foreground, on the occasion of the closure of the South Lancashire Transport Co and the end of trolleybus operation in 1958. *(EO coll)*

Facing page

A picturesque scene at Worsley Courthouse, just out of the picture but being served by the van – no doubt delivering food for a function. The photographer and his wife were among many couples whose wedding reception was held in this distinctive half-timbered building. The lowbridge Roe-bodied Guy trolleybus is *en route* to Atherton, and is about to negotiate the turning circle in the overhead for short workings to this point. Nowadays the constant roar from the traffic on the overbridge for the Lancashire Yorkshire motorway has spoiled the once-peaceful atmosphere as recorded here in 1957. *(JAS)*

Above

The oldest surviving Lancashire United vehicle is this 1930 Leyland LT1 Lion, 202, TF 818, which now resides in the Lincolnshire Vintage Vehicle Society's museum in Lincoln. It is in full running order and is seen operating a park-and-ride service during an open-day at a nearby military airfield. The bodywork is by Chas Roe. *(JAS, both)*

Number 53, one of the four Bolton-owned trolleybuses seen on a pleasant day in 1957 in the trolleybus terminus at Spinning Jenny Street, Leigh. Although the end of trolleybus operation was not far away it is still very smart and made an attractive subject for the photographer. Operated on the Leigh-Bolton service they were of highbridge configuration. To the right is the SLT logo carried by the trolleybuses, but never by the motor buses.
(JAS, both)

Another view in Worsley, this time with a Farnworth-bound 6-wheeled Guy BTX, again with Roe lowbridge bodywork. This one, No. 10, has been rebuilt by Bond of Wythenshawe as is clear from the revised front. *(JAS)*

Wartime Utility Sunbeam W number 63 at the Punchbowl office, on its way to Leigh and most likely returning from the Mosley Common pit on the service from there, but carrying shoppers at this time on a Saturday afternoon rather than miners. Leyland No. 53 waits its turn to proceed, also to Leigh, where the photographer was waiting for it. *(JAS)*

Contrasts in styling from Weymann's, above, with a lowbridge Dennis Lance, and Northern Counties, below, with a highbridge Guy Arab in the short-lived predominantly-red livery with grey roof. *(GL; STA)*

Not quite a matching pair, for the staircase position is now located at the front on the lower vehicle, to line up with its forward entrance. No. 271 has just come from the wash at Swinton depot. Above is No. 21, and both are Guy Arab Vs with Northern Counties highbridge bodywork. *(JAS, both)*

The railway lines and weeds tell their own story – Trafford Park with Daimler No. 12 and No. 36 behind it waiting to take workmen home on a Hollins Green service. *(GL)*

Fleetline No. 183 positively gleams in the sunshine as it stands outside the now-demolished Swinton depot; like Atherton it is now a housing development. *(JAS)*

Brand-new and just waiting to go into service from Atherton depot, is 33ft-long Daimler Fleetline No. 412. In the background, and also quite new, is one of the Plaxton-bodied Bristol RE models in its attractive reversed grey livery. *(JAS)*

A crew change is imminent as drivers and conductors make their way to the office just out of sight to the right. In the background the familiar chimney stands proudly alongside the road with its familiar lettering for all to see. *(JAS)*

Liverpool-bound AEC Reliance No. 5, now down-graded from coach duties to dual-purpose work. *(GL)*

Alexander-bodied Bristol RE number 295 leaves Eccles bus station on service 17. *(GL)*

Although the light grey and red livery was smart when new it soon faded – Bristol RE number 414 at Atherton. *(JAS)*

Leylands both by now – Leopard No. 440 from 1976 with Plaxton bodywork stands alongside 1977-built Leyland Fleetline No. 511 carrying the standard Northern Counties double-deck bodywork. Both are preserved.

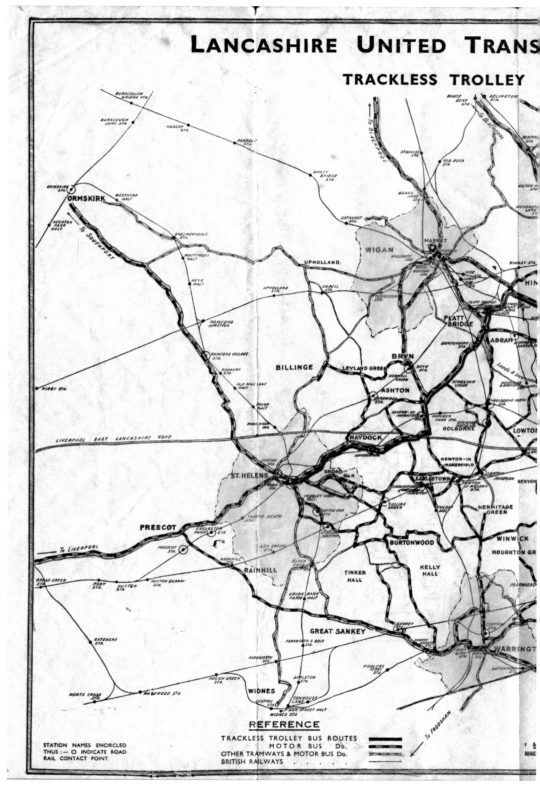

Courtesy Geoff Lumb and the Golcar Press.

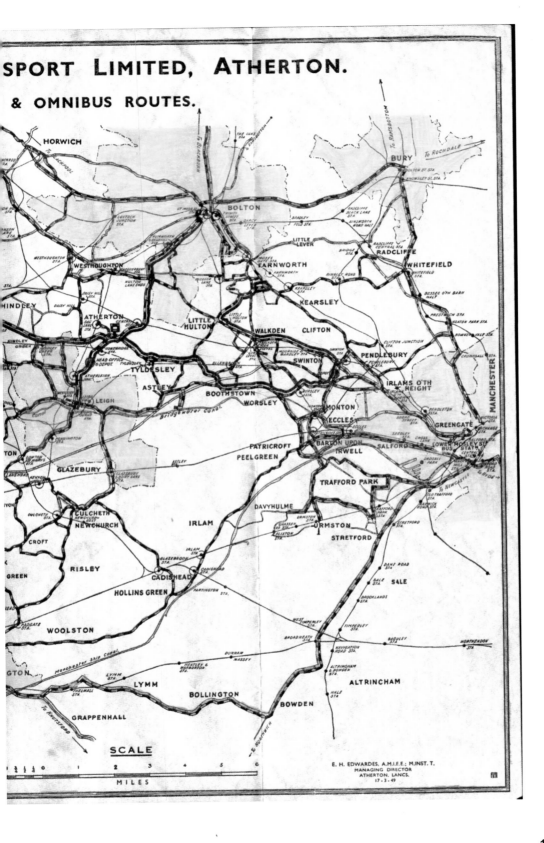

SPORT LIMITED, ATHERTON.

& OMNIBUS ROUTES.

SCALE

MILES

E. H. EDWARDES, A.M.I.E.E.; M.INST. T.
MANAGING DIRECTOR
ATHERTON, LANCS.
17-3-49

A fitting end to this section is provided by
this rural scene in Worsley, captured by
Steve Harrop.